THE
HARVEST
PANTRY

THE HARVEST PANTRY

Barbara Beckett

Photography by
Rodney Weidland

A Rathdowne Book
ALLEN & UNWIN

Measurements

Standard spoon and cup measurements are used in all the recipes. I recommend using a graduated nest of metric measuring cups: 1 cup, $^1/_2$ cup, $^1/_3$ cup and $^1/_4$ cup. The graduated nest of spoons comprises 1 tablespoon, 1 teaspoon, $^1/_2$ teaspoon and $^1/_4$ teaspoon. Use a standard litre or imperial pint measuring jug, which also shows cup measurements, for liquids. Spoon and cup measurements are level. Metric and imperial equivalents given are not exact, so follow either one or the other system of measurements within the recipe. Ovens should be preheated to the specified temperature.

Ingredients

Fresh **fruit** and **vegetables** should be used in the recipes unless otherwise stated. It is assumed they are washed. Size of vegetable is medium unless stated otherwise. **Herb** quantities are for fresh herbs; if they are unavailable, use half the quantity of dried herbs. Use freshly ground black **pepper** whenever pepper is listed; I always use sea salt (not iodised); use **salt** and pepper to individual taste. Use plain (all-purpose) **flour** otherwise stated. Fresh **ginger** should be used throughout, unless ground ginger is called for. Use fresh **chillies**; if substituting dried chillies, halve the quantity. I use cold-pressed virgin olive **oil**, but any type may be used. I always use fermented wine **vinegar**. Cider and malt vinegar may be substituted if preferred. White granulated **sugar** is used unless stated otherwise. **Vanilla sugar** is made by inserting a vanilla pod in a screw-topped jar of sugar.

For
Jean and Margaret

FRONT JACKET
An abundance of preserved and fresh foods. You always have plenty of food on hand when you preserve for rainy days.

TITLE PAGE
Pickled cucumbers with shallots and fennel. Use the recipe for Pickled Gherkins (page 71). A great standby to eat with cheese, meats and homely bread.

A Rathdowne Book
First published in 1993
Allen & Unwin Pty Ltd
9 Atchison Street
St Leonards, NSW 2065

Created and designed by
Barbara Beckett Publishing
14 Hargrave Street
Paddington, NSW 2021

© Barbara Beckett, 1993

National Library of Australia
Cataloguing-in-publication entry:
Beckett, Barbara
The harvest pantry
Includes index
ISBN 1 86373 5070
1. Cookery. 2. Gifts. I. Title

Edited by Deborah Conyngham
Photographs by Rodney Weidland
Designed by Amanda McPaul
and Barbara Beckett
Illustrated by Amanda McPaul
Typeset by Graphicraft Typesetters
Printed in Singapore

Contents

1 *The Harvest Pantry*

A well-stocked pantry is a treasure trove of food delights and a joy to see: garlands of garlic and onions; cured ham and strings of sausages; spicy chutneys and fruit jams; pickled onions and fresh cheese; bags of peas, beans and rice; boxes of sweets and rich fruit cake.

From earliest times, people have had to preserve food in seasons of abundance to supply the leaner months. They first learnt to dry meat and fish with strong winds. Later, after they learnt to cook with fire, meat and fish were salted and then smoked. Food was now being altered in taste as new flavours were created by the process of preservation itself. Preserving in pure fat, oil, sugar, wine and vinegar followed. Thousands of years later, we still preserve this way.

A pantry is an ancient tradition—and so is cooking by combining fresh ingredients with preserved foods and condiments. A pantry was normally a separate room, cool and dark, set aside for storing foodstuffs. It wasn't until very recently that the pantry was abandoned and packaged and fast food began to displace traditional habits. At the same time women aspired to work outside the home and an unsettling period for home-cooked food began. Ironically, scientists began studying human nutrition and began to realise that many of the old peasant cuisines were healthier for us.

I have tried to steer a steady course between the old pantry style of cooking and the needs of today. You can cook good, honest, homemade food with very little effort if you are prepared to spend some of your leisure hours making condiments and preserves. Make this an enjoyable occasion so it doesn't seem like work. We sit around the dining table near the kitchen and prepare our fruit and vegetables and chat or listen to music with a cup of tea, or a glass of wine occasionally. Sometimes a girlfriend comes around and we spend an afternoon making chutneys and pickles after a trip to the market. I swap condiments and preserves with friends. My retired father makes up all our Indian and Thai condiments. A gardening friend gives me fresh onions, garlic and bunches of unusual herbs so I can plait them and dry them. I will give him some of my liqueurs or olive paste in return.

The other change in our food habits has been the availability of foodstuffs from all over the world and the influence of other cultures on our eating. We now happily eat chicken curry with an Italian green salad and finish off with a Moroccan rice cake and no one will think it unusual—just delicious!

Cooking in a Hurry

Spontaneous and delicious meals can be prepared quickly and simply by combining fresh ingredients with pantry condiments and preserves. It may even be faster than driving to a takeaway. One thing I am sure of is that it is much cheaper and healthier. If you stock your refrigerator and freezer carefully and have a well-stocked pantry it takes no time at all to make a meal either directly from storage or combined with fresh ingredients.

A slice of basil butter on a char-grilled steak takes no time if you have the butter already made. Or perhaps you would prefer some pesto from the freezer instead. Prepare a tandoori chicken in a flash with Madrasi masala paste mixed with yoghurt as a marinade. Make a risotto from dried mushrooms, frozen peas and chicken stock. Take a fruit sorbet or parfait out of the freezer for dessert.

Don't worry if you haven't time to make all your own condiments and preserves. Use bought ones instead and your meals will be at least three quarters homemade. Fine cooking is an art and one we constantly practise and experiment with all our lives. Be adventurous and taste, taste, taste to find the exact proportions that appeal to your palate. Learn to trust your judgement and alter seasonings to suit yourself. Once you have mastered that, you need never be afraid of failures and can relax when creating new recipes.

Shopping

Trust your judgement when you go shopping. It is much more relaxing to look around to see what is in season, what is the freshest, or the best value, and let that decide your menu. It is quite thrilling to hold a tray of sun-ripened tomatoes in your arms and dream of all the possible things to make from it. Perhaps it is simply sliced tomatoes with a dribble of virgin olive oil and basil vinegar, a twist of pepper and some fresh cheese marinated in oil. Make a fresh tomato sauce with the rest of the tray and freeze what you don't eat. If you haven't much time, purée the tomatoes and freeze to make a pasta sauce, soup or sorbet later on.

Notes on Preserving

We are all part of a cycle of new life and growth, death and decay—a cycle of building up and breaking down. The food we eat is part of this and in preserving food we attempt to interrupt the breaking down part of the cycle. Food decomposition normally occurs through the action of enzymes, bacteria, yeast and moulds. When we preserve we need to eliminate these destructive agents and prevent their growth during storage. They can be destroyed by intense heat; drying by wind, sun or oven; freezing below 0°C (32°F); large quantities of sugar, salt, vinegar, oil or alcohol.

All ingredients should be as fresh as possible and free from blemishes. Wash meats, fruit and vegetables and dry with absorbent kitchen paper. Fruit and vegetables with skin on should be scrubbed. Whatever food item you are buying, there is no substitute for quality, so be a canny shopper, buy seasonally and keep an eye open for bargains.

When preserving fruit and vegetables, always use heavy-based saucepans lined with enamel, or stainless steel pans. It is better to cook in a larger pan than one that is too small. Stir with wooden spoons unless whisking.

When storing in jars, wash them thoroughly, preferably in the dishwasher. Always sterilise any container you wish to preserve food in. Put into the oven at 100°C (210°F) for 20 minutes. This applies to the condiments as well as jams and chutneys. You should be cooking in as clean and sterile a kitchen as you can manage in order to prevent those spoilage agents destroying your hard work.

Remember, when pouring a hot substance into a container, the container should be warm—otherwise it will shatter. Pack the food down well to expel any air bubbles that may harbour bacteria. Wipe clean any part of the jar or bottle not covered inside or outside. Once bottled, leave to cool down and keep covered with a clean tea-towel. When cold, seal the bottle.

Never forget to label. You will need to know the name of the recipe, the date made and when it will be ready to eat or when to use by. Use lined metal lids on acidic things like chutney and pickles. To be extra cautious, put a waxed disc over the surface of jams and preserves or pour a layer of paraffin wax over the top. Jam can have a paper cover but pickles and chutneys need lids. All items not refrigerated or frozen should be stored in a dark, ventilated, cool place—a cupboard, pantry or cellar.

If you have a cellar or equivalent and are the recipient of windfalls, you can keep fruits in cold storage by laying them on trays so they don't touch each

other, and stacking the trays so the air can circulate all around. Keep the room dark but well ventilated. Never wash anything before storing. Root vegetables can be stored in winter the same way, as can pumpkins and onions. Remove the husk from nuts and store in sacks or boxes.

There are tips for freezing scattered throughout the book. Look up the index for details.

Organising a Pantry

There is not much sense having a well-stocked pantry if it isn't organised. It will be easier to find your way, and for the family to follow, if things of a kind are stored together. There is nothing

ABOVE
A close-up of the makings for Puttanesca Sauce, a classic pasta sauce. Note the rich colour and texture of the Baked Tomato Sauce (page 34).

RIGHT
Eggplant Preserve (page 73) is very handy to have ready to use in a casserole or a vegetable curry. Cut thin slices to put on crusty bread with sun-dried tomatoes or fresh cheese.

more frustrating than constantly being asked where the lime pickle or the garam masala is.

For instance, keep all the grains such as rolled oats, rice and flour together; the oils and vinegars go together; sugar goes with salt; chutneys with jams and fruit preserves; dried fruit with nuts and seeds; pasta with noodles, and so forth.

Think of your pantry as a place of beauty; because, after all, that is where you are storing your wonderful jars and bottles of gleaming fruits and vegetables, your little bags of dried beans, peas and rice, bunches of herbs. Take pleasure in looking at it and thinking of all the fine eating to come. Rearrange it every now and then and discover that forgotten chutney, now matured for two years.

Do not despair if you haven't a romantic country cellar, designer store cupboard or old-fashioned walk-in pantry. Any old cupboard will do and even open shelving is fine as long as the food is not kept too long in the light. In fact, it does seem a shame to have such aesthetic things kept in the dark. The better looking bottles make a wonderful display on kitchen and dining room shelves.

A pantry can be an expression of creativity and love—love of food, and of friends and family who will share it with us. I hope you enjoy cooking from these recipes and eating homemade meals as much as we do.

Freezer Tip: Fruit and Vegetables. It makes sense to freeze if you haven't time to preserve a generous basket of tomatoes or a glut of strawberries. Either put them into the freezer whole; purée fruit ready for sauces, ice-cream or sorbets; blanch vegetables if you are going to keep them longer than 1 week.

What to Keep in a Pantry

This is a list of all the basic ingredients I have used in this book. They are all the foodstuffs that will last in your pantry. Your fresh food for the recipes in this book are additional. The index will help you find your way around the book. Of course, a pantry is a very personal choice and this is the one I have lived with for years. I admit I am never so organised or have enough space to manage all of this at the one time. So don't despair—just use this as an overall guide.

Oils and Vinegars
Extra virgin olive oil, olive oil, almond oil, walnut oil, peanut oil, mustard oil, herbed and spiced oils, red and white wine vinegar, champagne vinegar, sherry vinegar, Chinese and Japanese rice vinegar, apple cider vinegar, malt vinegar, balsamic vinegar and herbed and spiced vinegars.

Spices
Sea salt (fine and coarse), saltpetre, spiced and herbed salts, black peppercorns, Szechuan peppercorns, chilli powder, cayenne, paprika, chilli seeds, mustard seeds (black, brown and yellow), Dijon mustard (smooth and grainy), powdered mustard, whole cloves, whole nutmeg, cinnamon sticks, coriander seeds, juniper berries, cardamom pods and seeds, coriander seeds, cumin and black cumin seeds, fennel seeds, star anise, whole vanilla beans, sesame seeds, ground ginger, saffron threads, garlic powder, onion powder, fenugreek seeds, dried curry leaves, ground turmeric, laos powder, allspice berries, celery seeds, anise seeds, caraway seeds.

12

Dried Foods

Chillies, rosemary, savory, thyme, oregano, marjoram, bay leaves, sage, lemon grass, lavender, dried mushrooms, morel and dried porcini, prunes, dried apricots, peaches, apples, figs, raisins, sultanas, currants, citrus peel, glacé cherries, pineapple, pears, apricots, sunflower seeds, pumpkin seeds, sesame seeds, walnuts, hazelnuts, almonds (whole, slivered and ground), peanuts (fresh and unsalted), pine nuts, candlenuts, brazil nuts, pistachios, macadamias, chana dhal, split peas (toovar dhal), beans (cannellini, navy, flageolets, lima, red kidney, haricot, black-eyed, broad beans), lentils (small orange, small grey, large grey), chickpeas, cooking chocolate and powder.

Sugars, Cereals, etc.

Granulated sugar, caster sugar, icing sugar, brown sugar, dark brown sugar, scented sugars, honey, golden syrup, black treacle, plain flour (white and wholemeal), self-raising flour (white and wholemeal), cornflour, semolina and polenta, cracked wheat, couscous, barley, rolled oats, oat bran, wheatgerm, dried pasta, dried noodles, rice (short grain, long grain, Basmati, arborio, wild, brown, glutinous and jasmine), dried yeast, baking powder, bicarbonate of soda, gelatine, junket tablets (rennet), tea (Indian, Chinese and herbal), cocoa, dried skim milk.

Preserves

Capers, horseradish, gherkins, Chinese black beans, jam, redcurrant jelly, marmalade, jelly, conserves, chutney, pickles.

Condiments

Light soy sauce, nuoc mam (fish sauce), shrimp paste (blachan or kapee), Thai fish sauce (nam pla), Tabasco, tahini paste, hoisin sauce, orange flower water.

Canned Goods

Anchovies, tomatoes, tomato paste, tuna.

Long-Lasting Vegetables and Fruit

Lemon, lime, apples, oranges, fresh ginger, garlic, chillies, olives, coconut, onions, shallots, carrots, potatoes, parsnips, swedes, turnips, pumpkin.

Refrigerator

Unsalted butter, herbed and spiced butters, clarified butter, duck and goose fat, lard, parmesan cheese, pecorino cheese, gruyère cheese, mozzarella, fresh goat's cheese, fetta cheese, milk and cream, buttermilk, yoghurt, ham, bacon, prosciutto, sausage casings, cod's roe, eggs.

Freezer

Beef stock, chicken stock, coffee beans, peas, bread, breadcrumbs, sausages, rich shortcrust pastry, pâte brisée, puff pastry, bread dough, ice-cream, sorbet, parfaits.

Alcohol

Eau de vie, flavourless vodka, dry sherry, red and white wine, Madeira, port, rice wine, brandy, fruit liqueurs, gin, kirsch, white or dark rum, aquavit, calvados, framboise, slivovitz.

2 Condiments

$\mathcal{C}$ondiments —those aromatic flavourings that so enhance the taste of fresh homemade food—conjure up flavoured oils and vinegars, flavoured butters, spiced salts and scented sugars, mustards and horseradish, rich stock sauces, herbed mayonnaise and spicy fruit sauces and, of course, spice powders and pastes.

Condiments make it so simple to make a fine meal for your family or friends. All you need are the freshest and finest of ingredients, a few basic cooking techniques and a knowledge of condiments to flavour your food as it cooks or at the table.

Once you are familiar with these aromatic flavourings, it will expand your culinary repertoire a hundredfold and open up all types of exciting possibilities for that leg of lamb or mixed vegetable dish. It will make quick and easy meals possible while

Thai Chilli Dressing (page 20) is a dipping sauce for chicken and salad vegetables. Take a piece of chicken and some salad, sprinkle on some sauce, and roll it up in a lettuce leaf to eat. It's very relaxing to eat with your hands.

still being homemade. The leg of lamb can become a spicy Indian lamb curry with the addition of Madrasi masala paste, an Indonesian satay meal, a Thai red curry, lamb with chilli and black bean sauce or a Mexican chilli and orange dish. All the spicy tastes were already in your pantry—the hard work already done on a pleasurable rainy afternoon.

Flavoured Oils

A fine oil will enhance and compliment food, so it's well worth buying top quality oils. These are unrefined oils that have a good colour, a wonderful fragrance and a fine taste. They can be made from olives, almonds, walnuts and hazelnuts, peanuts, mustard and sesame seeds. I always aim to have these different oils in my pantry for variety. I use extra virgin and virgin olive oil and first pressing of the other oils. There is no substitute for quality, so shop around for your oil.

It makes sense to have a range of homemade flavoured oils in your pantry. It saves a lot of time if you can just sprinkle some basil oil onto a pasta dish or salad for extra flavour. Oils can be flavoured with fresh herbs, chilli, garlic, flowers and spices and then used in salad dressings and marinades, and for cooking and barbecuing.

Herb Oils

Use this basic recipe for flavouring oils with herbs such as thyme, tarragon, rosemary, bay leaf, or oregano.

> 1 cup fresh herbs
> 4 cups (1³/₄ imp. pts) extra virgin olive oil

Wash and dry the herbs and put into a wide-mouthed sterilised jar. Pour the oil over, seal and store in a cool dark place for three weeks. Strain the herbs off and pour the flavoured oil into sterilised bottles, seal and label. Decorate with a few twigs of the herb. Makes 4 cups.

Chilli Oil

> 1 cup (9 fl oz) first pressing peanut oil
> 20 small dried chillies
> 2 teaspoons Szechuan peppercorns
> 1 teaspoon sesame oil

Heat the peanut oil gently until it is warm but not boiling. Reduce the heat, add the chillies and peppercorns. Cook until the chillies turn black. Remove from heat, cover and cool. Add the sesame oil and pour into a wide-mouthed jar. Strain the oil after 24 hours into a sterilised bottle. Keep refrigerated in a hot climate. Makes 1 cup.

Garlic Oil

Delicious sprinkled on bread and pizzas, salad and warm vegetables.

> 6 garlic cloves
> 1 cup (9 fl oz) extra virgin oil

Bruise the garlic, by pressing with the blade of a knife, and peel. Put into a saucepan with the oil and heat until it is aromatic and blood temperature. Remove from heat and allow to cool. Pour into a sterilised bottle. Makes 1 cup.

Flavoured Vinegars

*H*erb, fruit and flower vinegars have been made for hundreds of years for medicinal purposes and to flavour food and drinks. The principal flavouring ingredients to use are thyme, basil, tarragon, marjoram, oregano, chives, dill, fennel, rosemary, sage, savory, mint, shallots, garlic, chilli, peppercorns, juniper berries, raspberries, strawberries, blackberries, pears, cherries, lavender, violets, nasturtium flowers, rose petals and carnations. It is also interesting to experiment with several kinds of herbs instead of a single one—it usually makes a more complex aromatic flavour. Always buy a good quality wine vinegar such as red or white wine vinegar, champagne or sherry vinegar. Other vinegars handy to have in your pantry are Chinese and Japanese rice vinegars, apple cider vinegar, malt vinegar and balsamic vinegar. Use flavoured vinegars to sprinkle on fresh strawberries or fruit salad; a dash in mineral water with a sliver of lemon peel makes a refreshing drink; use as a dip for oysters and prawns or as a marinade for barbecuing fish and meats; add a dash to soups or sauces to give a sweet and sour flavour; sprinkle flavoured vinegar with oil for a simple and tasty salad dressing; use instead of salt and be healthier. Flavoured vinegars are quick and easy to make, they look most attractive and, of course, they are so much cheaper than the bottles you buy. Use the following recipe as a basis for other flavoured vinegars.

Nasturtium Vinegar

This vinegar has a refreshing nutty flavour. Within four hours, the vinegar will have taken on the glorious colour of the petals you have chosen, so only use one colour at a time.

1 cup nasturtium flowers
3 cups (26 fl oz) white wine vinegar

*W*ash and dry the flowers and pack into a wide-mouthed jar. Pour the vinegar over. Leave in a dark place for 2 weeks. Strain into a sterilised bottle and label. Do not add flowers as they tend to disintegrate, but if you are flavouring with herbs put a sprig into the bottle to make it look more attractive and to remind you what kind of vinegar it is. Makes 3 cups.

Hot Sherry Vinegar

Try this sprinkled on fish or as a dipping sauce for prawns and oysters.

10 red chillies
10 black peppercorns
1 cup (9 fl oz) sherry vinegar

*W*ash and dry the chillies and put into a sterilised bottle with the peppercorns. Pour the vinegar over, seal and label. It will take a week to mature. No need to strain. Makes 1 cup.

Tarragon Vinegar

3 cups (26 fl oz) wine vinegar
4 shallots
6 stalks of tarragon
1$^1/_2$ tablespoons yellow mustard seeds

*W*arm the vinegar to blood heat. Slightly bruise the shallots with the blade of a knife and peel. Wash and dry the tarragon. Put all the ingredients into a sterilised jar and seal. Strain after 6 weeks into a sterilised bottle and add a fresh tarragon stalk for decoration. Makes 3 cups.

Salad Dressings

There are as many ways of making a salad dressing as there are varieties of salad. The proportion of oil to vinegar tends to be very personal—3 parts of oil to 1 part of vinegar or 5 to one? It also depends on the fruitiness of the oil and kind of vinegar used. Keep tasting the dressing until the proportion is right for your palate. Experiment with flavoured oils and vinegars, fresh herbs and flowers. Always use the highest quality ingredients. These dressings will also make excellent marinades for barbecuing meats and seafood.

Vinaigrette

This classic French dressing is perfect for most salads. You can use lemon juice instead of vinegar if you are drinking fine wine with the salad. A tablespoon of capers can make a pleasant addition.

  3 tablespoons extra virgin olive oil
  1 tablespoon wine vinegar
  2 teaspoons Dijon mustard
  1 teaspoon salt, optional

*P*ut all the ingredients into a bottle and shake well. Keep in the coldest part of the fridge until needed so the mustard and oil can emulsify. Serves 6.

Italian Dressing

The Italians like to dress their salad individually at the table just before eating. They place little flasks or bottles of virgin olive oil and balsamic vinegar as well as pepper and salt on the table.

Flavoured vinegars capture the summer goodness to enjoy all year round. From the left, Nasturtium Vinegar (page 17), Raspberry Salad Dressing (this page), Rosemary Vinegar (page 17), Hot Sherry Vinegar (page 17) and Blackberry Vinegar (page 17).

Each person dresses their salad according to their preference. The flasks have very thin spouts so the oil and vinegar can dribble over the salad. If you do not have flasks, cut a small wedge out of the cork of the bottle, lift the cork almost out and dribble the oil through the space. Balsamic vinegar is an aged vinegar much prized for its delicious flavour. It must be aged for at least 10 years and some are aged for 50 years or more. Only a very few drops are needed, so don't faint when you see how expensive it is. I am told there are more family disputes in Italy over who inherits the family barrel of aceto balsamico than about anything else!

Moroccan Salad Dressing

Dress a tomato salad or mesclun, or use it to marinate kebabs and grilled fish.

  3 garlic cloves
  2 tablespoons lemon juice
  6 tablespoons virgin olive oil
  $1/2$ teaspoon chopped chilli
  3 tablespoons fresh coriander leaves
  Pepper and salt, optional

*R*oast the garlic cloves, peel and mash them. Place all the ingredients in a jar and shake well. Refrigerate until needed. Serves 6.

Raspberry Salad Dressing

A lovely dressing for a chicken salad or poured over fresh fruits with soft cheese.

  $1/2$ punnet raspberries
  3 tablespoons olive oil
  Juice of 1 lemon
  2 teaspoons strawberry liqueur
  Pepper and salt

*W*ash the raspberries and blend to a purée. Put all the ingredients into a bottle and shake well. Serves 6.

Chinese Salad Dressing

Use this to dress a salad or to marinate chicken or pork before grilling.

1 garlic clove, crushed and skinned
1 teaspoon grated fresh ginger
1 tablespoon finely sliced spring
  onion
1 tablespoon light soy sauce
1 tablespoon wine vinegar
1 tablespoon dry sherry
4 tablespoons peanut oil
1 teaspoon Szechuan peppercorns

*C*ombine all the ingredients in a screw-top jar and shake vigorously. Store in the refrigerator until needed. Serves 6.

Thai Chilli Dressing

This dressing is very pleasant tossed over a mixed salad of leaves or as a dipping sauce. It blends well with pork and chicken.

3 garlic cloves, mashed and finely
  chopped
3 red chillies, mashed and finely
  chopped
Juice of 3 lemons
5 tablespoons Thai fish sauce
5 tablespoons peanut oil
1 teaspoon sesame oil
Pepper

*C*ombine all the ingredients and shake well. Refrigerate until required. Serves 6.

Vietnamese Salad Dressing

1 medium red onion, finely sliced
3 garlic cloves, mashed and finely
  sliced
5 tablespoons rice vinegar or wine
  vinegar
1 tablespoon nuoc mam
  (fish sauce)
1 tablespoon light soy sauce
5 tablespoons peanut oil
Pepper
$^{1}/_{2}$ teaspoon honey

*C*ombine all the ingredients in a screw-top jar and shake vigorously.

Butters

*F*lavoured butters can be used as small pats to give a finishing flavour to grilled meat or fish, as a final enrichment for a sauce or as a spread for a simple starter. It is very handy to have some ready in the refrigerator or freezer to quickly season a meal. Use the basic recipe for fines herbes butter to make the following interesting combinations.*

Fines Herbes Butter

125 g (4 oz) unsalted butter at
  room temperature
1 tablespoon lemon juice
2 tablespoons finely chopped chives,
  parsley, tarragon and thyme
Pepper

*C*ream the butter then gradually beat in the lemon juice, the herbs and pepper. Form the mixture into a log and wrap securely in aluminium foil. Either store for a week in the refrigerator or freeze. Cut off slices as needed and put a pat on meats and fish or toss with steamed vegetables. Makes 12 slices.

Variation: To use as a starter add a little olive oil at the end of the creaming to help smooth the mixture. Pack it into a small pot or a jar and chill or freeze.

Herb Butters
Try herbs such as basil, tarragon, mint, dill, oregano, thyme or sage, on their own or in combination.

Ravigote Butter
Add 1 finely chopped shallot to basic recipe. Blanch the herbs and shallot for several minutes, drain and pat dry.

Garlic Butter
Add 3 crushed and chopped garlic cloves to basic recipe. Eat also on warm bread and potatoes baked in their skins.

Mustard Butter
Add 2 tablespoons Dijon mustard or grainy mustard instead of herbs to basic recipe. Replace the lemon juice with 1 tablespoon of white wine.

Anchovy Butter
Add 10 anchovy fillets instead of herbs to basic recipe.

Black Olive Butter
Add 2 tablespoons of finely chopped olive pulp instead of herbs in basic recipe.

Chilli and Coriander Butter
Replace herbs in basic recipe with fresh coriander (cilantro) and add 2 red chillies, finely chopped. Lovely with chicken.

Orange Butter
Replace herbs and lemon juice in basic recipe with grated peel of one orange and 1 tablespoon of orange juice. Excellent with fish.

Montpellier Butter

Slightly more time consuming to make than the other recipes, this compound butter is excellent with baked and poached eggs.

> 250 g (8 oz) butter at room
>   temperature
> 2 hard-boiled eggs, sieved
> 2 tablespoons olive oil
> 2 garlic cloves, crushed
> 1 cup shredded lettuce leaves
> 1 cup spinach leaves
> 1/2 cup watercress sprigs
> 1 tablespoon parsley
> 2 shallots, finely chopped
> 2 tablespoons capers
> 1 teaspoon Dijon mustard
> 2 tablespoons lemon juice
> Pepper

Cream the butter, eggs, oil and garlic. Blanch the lettuce, spinach, watercress, parsley and shallots, drain and pat dry. Finely chop them and add them to the capers, mustard, lemon juice and pepper. Combine with the creamed butter. Roll into a log and wrap in aluminium foil. Makes 24 slices.

Clarified Butter

Clarified butter is pure butter fat with the milk solids and impurities removed. This will allow butter fat to reach a higher temperature when cooked, which is necessary when frying. You can make up this quantity and store it in the refrigerator until needed. It lasts indefinitely.

200 g (7 oz) unsalted butter

Melt the butter gently and allow to simmer but not to burn. It is ready when the top is translucent and the solids are on the bottom. Remove from heat, rest until warm and strain into bowl through a layer of muslin in a fine sieve. Refrigerate.

21

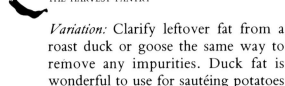

Variation: Clarify leftover fat from a roast duck or goose the same way to remove any impurities. Duck fat is wonderful to use for sautéing potatoes and to make hearty winter casseroles.

Smen

In Morocco they use smen instead of butter. A similar version is easily made and will keep for up to 6 months in the refrigerator.

> *250 g (8 oz) unsalted butter, diced*
> *1 cup (9 fl oz) olive oil*
> *1 tablespoon salt*
> *¹/₄ teaspoon Herbes de Provence (page 86)*

Melt the butter and oil and slowly bring it to the boil. Let it simmer without stirring for 30 minutes or until the butter has separated, clear on top and solids on the bottom. Sprinkle in the salt and herbs. Spoon off the clear liquid into a sterilised pot or jar. Cover and refrigerate when cold.

Spiced Salts

Spiced and herbed salts have been a traditional method of flavouring and preserving food for thousands of years in cuisines where it was necessary to preserve food at its peak for the necessities of the table in leaner months. It still makes sense to use these delicious concoctions for casseroles and terrines, salting a leg of pork or ham, or adding flavour to barbecued meat and vegetables. They are a good item to have on hand in the kitchen for a quick and tasty improvement to chops or sausages. Just run your eye down the list of spice ingredients in a recipe or decide to substitute with one of these combinations. Store in airtight jars in the refrigerator or freezer.

Sel Epicé

A spicy seasoning salt for terrines, casseroles and large meat dishes. Store in airtight jars. Make some for yourself and give some away as gifts.

> *3 bay leaves*
> *1 cup (7 oz) sea salt*
> *3 tablespoons peppercorns, finely ground*
> *2 tablespoons ground cloves*
> *2 tablespoons ground nutmeg*
> *1 tablespoon ground cinnamon*
> *1 tablespoon ground coriander seeds*
> *1 tablespoon ground thyme*

Break the bay leaves into small pieces and put them with all the other ingredients into the food processor and blend. Makes 2 cups.

Herbed Salt

Use this aromatic mixture of herbs and salt to add flavour to grilled chicken, lamb and pork as well as hearty vegetables such as potatoes and pumpkins.

> *1 tablespoon dried rosemary, finely ground*
> *1 tablespoon marjoram, finely ground*
> *2 dried bay leaves, crumbled*
> *1 teaspoon ground pepper*
> *¹/₂ teaspoon cayenne*
> *¹/₂ cup (4 oz) sea salt*

Mix all the ingredients together. Pass through a fine sieve and seal in a screw-top jar. Makes ²/₃ cup.

Flavoured butters last for months in the refrigerator and are a great stand-by to flavour grilled meats and fish. Spread on fresh crusty bread for a treat. From the left, Chilli and Coriander Butter (page 21), Black Olive Butter (page 21) and Orange Butter (page 21).

Aromatic Salt

An equal mixture of spices and salt make a fascinating mixture for experimenting with terrines and meat dishes in your cooking repertoire.

> $^1/_2$ cup (4 oz) sea salt
> 2 teaspoons cayenne
> 1 tablespoon nutmeg
> 1 tablespoon cinnamon
> 1 tablespoon cloves
> 1 tablespoon ground oregano
> 1 tablespoon ground basil
> 1 tablespoon ground sage
> 6 dried bay leaves, crumbled

Grind all the spices to a fine powder. Pass through a sieve and seal in a screw-top jar. Makes 1 cup.

Flavoured Salt for Salting Meat

See the recipes on page 135 and page 136 for using this salt when brining meat.

> $2^1/_2$ cups ($1^1/_2$ lb) salt
> 3 cloves
> 1 teaspoon salt
> 3 tablespoons juniper berries
> 6 bay leaves
> $^1/_2$ cup dried thyme leaves

Mix all ingredients together well and store hermetically until needed. Makes enough for 3 kg (6 lb) meat.

Freezer Tip: Meat. Freezing will never improve the taste of meat, so only do it if necessary. Pack into a good quality polythene bag and make sure there is as little air as possible. Thaw for 24 hours in the refrigerator. I make sure lots of aromatic herbs and spices are used in long, slow cooking to make up for the loss of quality.

Dry Spices from Morocco

Use in the cooking of hearty dishes or as a condiment on the table to add extra flavour to soups, grills and vegetable dishes.

> 1 tablespoon dried lavender, crumbled
> 1 tablespoon dried rosemary
> 2 tablespoons thyme
> 1 tablespoon chilli powder
> 1 tablespoon ground cardamom
> 1 tablespoon ground cinnamon
> 1 tablespoon ground cloves
> 2 tablespoons ground coriander
> 2 tablespoons ground pepper
> 2 tablespoons ground nutmeg
> 2 tablespoons ground cumin

Grind all the ingredients and mix well together. Store in a screw-top jar. Makes $1^1/_3$ cups.

Five-Spice Salt

A well-known Chinese condiment to use as a dip for roasted meats or to sprinkle on stir-fry dishes.

> 3 tablespoons ground Szechuan peppercorns
> 2 tablespoons ground cinnamon
> 2 teaspoons ground fennel seeds
> 2 teaspoons ground star anise
> 2 teaspoons ground cloves
> $^1/_2$ cup (4 oz) salt

Mix all the spices together well to make five-spice powder. Heat a wok or pan and pour in salt. Keep stirring until salt is well heated. Cool for 5 minutes then stir in the five-spice powder. Store in a screw-top jar.

Scented Sugars

*T*hese aromatic sugars only take a few minutes to make but will give great pleasure. A sniff of the jar when you open it will remind you of the fragrant perfumes of spring or summer. The sugars only take two weeks for the herbs or flowers to penetrate. Use the basic method for violet sugar to make other flavours such as lavender flower sugar, rose petal, scented geranium leaves, rosemary, lemon balm, bay leaves and peppermint. Use these flavoured sugars for custards, ice-creams, biscuits and cakes. The recipe for vanilla sugar is on page 4.

Violet Sugar

$^1/_2$ cup of violet flowers, washed and dried
3 cups (1$^1/_2$ lb) caster sugar

*L*ay the flowers on a piece of brown paper for 24 hours in a warm place so they begin to dry. Place the flowers and sugar in alternate layers in a clean jar. It will be ready in 2 weeks. The flowers can be sifted if liked or left in the jar to remind you of their beauty. Remove the flowers when cooking with the sugar. Makes 3$^1/_4$ cups.

Thyme-Scented Honey

Use your imagination to add different herbs to honey. They look especially lovely when in flower.

10 sprigs of thyme
500 g (1 lb) clear honey

*S*imply immerse the thyme in a jar of warm honey that you have left in blood-temperature water for half an hour.

Vanilla Essence

It is very expensive to buy natural vanilla essence so why not make your own? If you can get eau de vie it is best as it has no flavour.

2 vanilla beans, split and cut in half
1 cup (9 fl oz) eau de vie or vodka

*P*ut the vanilla into a bottle with the spirit. Seal and store in a dark place for two months. Use drop by drop as for vanilla extract. Makes 1 cup.

Coconut Milk

You can make coconut milk from freshly grated coconut and freeze the leftover grated coconut or milk if the whole quantity isn't required. Preparing your own makes an amazing difference to the taste of Asian food and it is not hard work if you make a large quantity ready for the next few dishes.

When buying a coconut, shake it to make sure it has plenty of liquid in it and is therefore fresh. Crack it in half. (The liquid isn't used except for a drink.) Prise the coconut flesh from the skin and wash. Grate the flesh in the food processor. Freeze what isn't required for immediate recipe.

1$^1/_4$ cups (11 fl oz) boiling water
2 cups (6 oz) grated coconut

*P*our water over the coconut and let it sit for 5 minutes. Strain it through a piece of muslin lining a sieve. Press well to squeeze out all the liquid. This milk is known as thick coconut milk. Makes 1$^1/_2$ cups.

For thin coconut milk repeat the process twice using the pulp left from the thick coconut milk. Makes 1$^1/_2$ cups.

Mustards

*I*t isn't difficult at all to make your own mustards, whether straight from seeds or by flavouring a ready-made Dijon mustard. Mustards are basically a paste made from mustard seeds and flavoured with herbs or spices, sugar, vinegar or wine. Mustard pastes will last for months but I've also included some mustard sauces to prepare straight from your pantry with the addition of fresh herbs. All the mustards mentioned will also make excellent marinades for meats and strongly flavoured fish.

There are three types of mustard seeds: 'nigra', or black, mustard is the most pungent; 'juncea', or brown, mustard is not quite as strong; 'alba', or white, mustard has the mildest flavour.

Hot Honey Mustard

This is excellent with ham, corned beef or cheddar cheese. If you don't have a food mill to crush the mustard, be old-fashioned and use a mortar and pestle.

$^1/_2$ *cup (3 oz) black mustard seeds*
$^1/_2$ *cup (5 oz) honey*
3 tablespoons wine vinegar

*C*rush the mustard seeds to a powder in a food mill. Heat the honey in a pan until it begins to change colour. Add the mustard and mix well. Slowly stir in the vinegar bit by bit until it is a smooth paste. Pour into a sterilised jar and seal. Makes $1^1/_4$ cups.

Sesame Mustard

A very nice nutty mustard. Spread some over chicken pieces before grilling—delicious!

$^2/_3$ *cup (4 oz) brown mustard seeds*
$^1/_2$ *cup (3 oz) sesame seeds*
1 teaspoon sea salt, optional
$1^1/_2$ *cups (12 fl oz) unsweetened white grape juice or wine*

*M*ix all the ingredients together and allow to soak for 24 hours. In the food processor, blend just enough to lightly break up the seeds. Add more grape juice if it is too thick. Put into pots or jars and leave for two weeks to mature. Makes $2^1/_2$ cups.

Sweet Ginger Mustard

1 cup (5 oz) brown mustard seeds
4 tablespoons wine vinegar
$^1/_4$ *teaspoon chilli powder*
2 tablespoons finely chopped ginger
1 tablespoon honey
$^1/_2$ *teaspoon salt, optional*

*C*rush the mustard seeds in a food mill. Soak the mustard powder in the vinegar for 12 hours. Put all the ingredients into the food processor and blend until you have a smooth paste. Makes 1 cup.

Tarragon Mustard

Experiment with other herbs such as thyme, mint and rosemary for variations. Add garlic or ginger.

$1^1/_2$ *cups (8 oz) yellow mustard seeds*
1 cup (9 fl oz) white wine vinegar
2 tablespoons chopped tarragon
1 cup (9 fl oz) olive oil
2 tablespoons sugar

Coconut Milk (page 25) is easy to make yourself and does taste better made with the freshly grated fruit. Just be sure you have a very strong person handy to crack that coconut in the first place!

Grind the mustard seeds in a food mill. Soak the mustard powder in the vinegar for 12 hours. Combine all the ingredients in the food processor and blend to a smooth paste. Pack into sterilised pots or jars and allow to mature for 2 weeks. Makes 3 cups.

Five-Minute Flavoured Mustards

If you don't want to go the bother of grinding your own mustard seeds you can flavour either a prepared Dijon mustard, smooth or grainy. Use this recipe as a basic guide to follow. Eat about an hour after making it to catch it at its peak.

> 1/2 cup (3 oz) Dijon mustard
> 1 tablespoon finely chopped basil
> 1 teaspoon wine vinegar

Stir all the ingredients until you have a smooth paste. Return to mustard pot. Makes 1/2 cup.
Variations:

Olive Mustard
Add 3 tablespoons of finely chopped green or black olives to the basic recipe instead of the basil. Great with grilled steak or chops.

Lime Mustard
Add 1 tablespoon of grated lime zest and two tablespoons of lime juice to basic recipe instead of basil and vinegar.

Dill Mustard
Add 2 tablespoons of dill instead of basil and 2 teaspoons of honey to the basic recipe. This is wonderful with fish, poultry and potatoes.

Sauces

Stocks
A fine stock is the basis of many sauces such as sauce espagnole or brown sauce; it is also the foundation of many soups. Stocks will last four days in the refrigerator or up to three months in the freezer. Get into the habit of making stock in bulk and freezing it after you have removed the fat. For small quantities it is a good idea to put some of the stock into ice cube trays, freeze, then store the cubes in plastic bags in the freezer. Don't forget to label.

Rich Beef Stock

1 tablespoon butter
2 onions, chopped
2 carrots, chopped
1 kg (2 lb) shin of beef, cut into 4 pieces
2/3 cup (6 fl oz) red wine
Bouquet Garni (page 88)
1 tablespoon peppercorns
3 cloves
1 knuckle of veal, cut into 3 pieces
1 chicken carcase

Melt the butter and sauté the onions and carrots until onions are golden. Add the beef and brown all over. Pour in the red wine, the bouquet garni, peppercorns and cloves. Bring to the boil. Transfer to a large stock pot and add the veal and chicken. Cover with water and simmer very slowly for about 6 hours. Strain and refrigerate. Remove the fat from the surface when it has set on top of the stock.

Chicken Stock

For this light stock use chicken carcases or an old boiling fowl. I freeze my chicken carcases and make stock when I find I have

*three in the freezer. The veal bones provide
gelatine and a richer texture.*

> 1.25 kg (2¹/₂ lb) chicken bones and
>   veal bones
> 1 teaspoon peppercorns
> 1 onion
> 1 carrot
> Several stalks of celery
> Bouquet Garni (page 88)
> 1 teaspoon salt, optional

*P*ut all the ingredients except the salt
into a large pan. Pour in enough water
to just cover the bones. Bring to the
boil slowly and keep skimming the surface, removing all the scum. Simmer
gently for three hours. Add salt to taste.
Strain the stock into a bowl and when
cool refrigerate. When the fat has set
solid on the surface remove it. Freeze if
not required within 5 days.

Consommé

> 3 eggwhites and shells, crumbled
> 100 g (3 oz) minced topside beef
> 1 onion, chopped
> 1 carrot, chopped
> 1 stalk celery, chopped
> 3 stalks parsley
> 1 leek, chopped
> 5 cups (2¹/₄ imp. pts) Rich Beef
>   Stock (page 28)
> Pepper and salt
> 4 tablespoons port

*P*ut the eggwhites and shells into the
stock pot. Beat with a whisk, then add
the meat and vegetables. Pour in the
stock and bring slowly to the boil, stirring all the time. As soon as it is boiling
reduce heat to simmering. The egg
white will rise to the top bringing the
scum with it. After 15 minutes season
to your taste and strain the stock
through a layer of muslin over a fine
sieve. Before serving, add the port and

heat the consommé until nearly boiling. Garnish with chives or watercress.
Makes 4 cups.

Meat Glaze (Glace de Viande)

*T*his is a bit like having homemade
stock cubes at hand, only vastly superior. You can use this essence to
create instant sauces or soups as above.
Simply reduce two cups of consommé
until it becomes syrupy. When it cools
it will be a thick rubbery consistency.
Put into a small sterilised jar and store
in the refrigerator. Makes ¹/₂ cup.

Brown Sauce

*This is the handiest and tastiest of sauces to
use on steak and chops or any elegant beef
dish. It keeps well in the refrigerator. (Even
after freezing, it tastes reasonable—though
not as luscious.)*

> 2 tablespoons oil
> 1¹/₂ tablespoons flour
> 2¹/₄ cups (1 imp. pts) Rich Beef
>   Stock (page 28)
> 1 tablespoon tomato paste
> Bouquet Garni (page 88)
> 1 teaspoon peppercorns
> 1 teaspoon salt

Freezer Tip: Curries and casseroles. It can
save a lot of effort to make a large
quantity and freeze some for later use.
Highly spiced and tasty casseroles are
best for freezing. Only cook for three-
quarters of the time and make sure there
is plenty of sauce to cover the meat.
Freeze when cool. When wanted, take
out of the freezer and preferably let sit
in the refrigerator for 24 hours before
using.

Heat the oil in a heavy pan and blend in the flour. Cook gently until a good brown. Remove from the heat and add $1^3/_4$ cups stock. Bring to the boil, stirring well, and add remaining ingredients. Half cover with a lid and simmer gently for about 25 minutes. Add the remaining stock, bring to a rapid boil. Remove from heat, and take off the scum that comes to the surface. Strain through a fine sieve. Makes $1^1/_2$ cups.

Sauce Madère

Add 3 tablespoons of Madeira to 1 cup of Brown Sauce. Heat and serve.

Aux Fines Herbes

1 cup finely chopped fines herbes (parsley, chives, tarragon and watercress),
$^1/_2$ cup (4 oz) white wine
1 cup Brown Sauce (sauce espagnole)

Put the herbs and wine in pan and boil down until there is hardly any liquid left. Add the brown sauce and cook gently for five minutes. Strain and serve the sauce with a small fresh sprinkling of herbs. Makes 1 cup.

Mayonnaise

A classic homemade mayonnaise is the basis of a myriad of sauces since all kinds of combinations of herbs and flavourings can be added to make it more suitable for particular dishes. Use also as a dip with crudités

or toast. *If the mayonnaise curdles, put a fresh egg yolk in a clean bowl and start again, dripping the curdled mayonnaise in drop by drop. The basic sauce will keep in a screw-top jar in the refrigerator for two weeks. Your kitchen equipment must be spotless, the eggs fresh and at room temperature and you must be careful to only add the oil drop by drop at the beginning of the liaison. It is quite magical to make the first time.*

2 egg yolks
1 teaspoon Dijon mustard
$^1/_4$ teaspoon salt
1 cup (9 fl oz) olive oil
1 tablespoon lemon juice

Beat together the egg yolks, mustard and salt. Add the oil, drop by drop, beating all the time. You can use a whisk, an electric beater or a food processor. As the mayonnaise thickens, you can add the oil in larger quantities. When thick, add the lemon juice and stir in with a wooden spoon. You may need to add more lemon juice or hot water after it has been stored for a while as it will thicken up again. Makes 1 cup.
Variations: Vary the type of oil and herbs used, add Olive Paste (page 77), horseradish, Fresh Tomato Sauce (page 32), or anchovies.

Mayonnaise Suédoise

Wonderful with pork, ham and duck.

$^1/_2$ cup (5 oz) mayonnaise
$^1/_2$ cup (1 oz) cold apple purée
2 teaspoons horseradish

Mix the ingredients together and chill until serving. Makes 1 cup.

A classic sauce to serve with meat, Sauce Madère (this page) is hard to beat for flavour with a nice thick, juicy steak. The basis is Rich Beef Stock (page 28) and there are no short cuts.

Sauce Tartare

The classic sauce for any kind of fish or shellfish. Homemade is infinitely superior to bought.

    1 cup (10 oz) mayonnaise
    1 tablespoon finely chopped shallots
    1 tablespoon chopped fines herbes
      or parsley
    1 tablespoon capers
    2 tablespoons gherkins

Combine the ingredients and chill until serving. Makes $1\frac{1}{4}$ cups.

Sauce Verte

This is wonderful with cold meats or as a dip.

    1 cup of mixed herbs such as
      tarragon, chervil, sorrel, chives,
      parsley or spinach

Blanch the herbs for two minutes, dry and chop finely. Mix with the mayonnaise. Chill until serving. Makes $1\frac{1}{4}$ cups.

Aïoli

A marvellous pungent sauce or dip for an alfresco lunch.

    4 garlic cloves
    1 cup (10 oz) mayonnaise

Press the garlic cloves with the back of a knife. Peel them and then pound them in a mortar and pestle until creamy. Combine with the mayonnaise and chill until serving. Makes 1 cup.

Freezer Tip: Keeping coffee beans in a screw-top jar in the freezer is the best way to keep them fresh.

Tomato Sauces

Most people never tire of tomato sauce especially if it is homemade. Tomato sauce is one of the handiest sauces to have in your pantry as it goes with practically everything. I have included five recipes which vary considerably. Some need to be eaten straight away, some are suitable for freezing, others are pickled or preserved with oil and can be stored in the pantry cupboard. Always use very ripe tomatoes.

Fresh Tomato Sauce

    2 kg (4 lb) tomatoes
    3 tablespoons olive oil
    2 onions, sliced
    6 garlic cloves, chopped
    $\frac{1}{2}$ cup basil, finely chopped
    Pepper and salt
    Basil leaves to garnish
    Olive oil

Pour boiling water over the tomatoes and let them sit for 10 minutes. Skin them and roughly chop them. Heat the oil in the pan and add the onions. Cook until transparent then add the garlic for a minute. Stir in the tomatoes and basil, bring to the boil and let the sauce simmer slowly for an hour or longer until most of the moisture has evaporated. Season with salt and pepper. Pour into sterilised jars or bottles, making sure you dispel any air bubbles. Leave room at the top to place a basil leaf and a layer of oil to seal the sauce. When you open a bottle replace the oil layer and store in the refrigerator. Makes 4 cups.

Spicy Tomato Sauce (page 34) on the left and the preparation for making it. Note the homemade Garam Masala (page 46) in the glass jar which will save time when seasoning.

Tomato Coulis

This makes a wonderful fresh sauce for all kinds of pasta and grilled or steamed meat, seafood and vegetables. It will last about a week in the refrigerator and it also freezes well. Add Chicken Stock (page 28) to make a soup in an instant or Yoghurt (page 149) to make a chilled soup.

> 1 kg (2 lb) tomatoes
> 3 tablespoons virgin olive oil
> 1 shallot, finely chopped
> Bouquet Garni (page 88)
> Salt and pepper

Peel the tomatoes, skin, expel the seeds and roughly chop. Put the oil and shallot into the pan and cook until the shallot is transparent. Add the tomatoes and bouquet garni and cook for twenty minutes only. Remove from heat, take out bouquet garni and blend sauce in the food processor. Season with salt and pepper. Makes 2$^1/_2$ cups.

Spicy Tomato Sauce

A nice large quantity to make as it will last for a year. Make when there is a glut of tomatoes at the market or in your garden.

> 4 kg (8 lb) tomatoes, peeled and
>   chopped
> 5 onions, sliced
> 10 garlic cloves, crushed
> 1 teaspoon cayenne
> 1 tablespoon pepper
> 2 tablespoons Garam Masala
>   (page 46)
> 1 teaspoon ground cloves
> 4$^1/_2$ cups (2 imp. pts) wine vinegar
> 1 cup (8 oz) sugar
> 2 teaspoons salt

Put the tomatoes, onions and garlic into a large saucepan and simmer for 3 hours. Leave overnight. Blend the

mixture in the food processor and put back into the saucepan. Tie up the spices in a muslin bag and add to the mixture with the vinegar, sugar and salt. Bring to the boil and simmer for about an hour or until the sauce is thick. Remove the spices. Ladle the sauce into warm, sterilised bottles, seal with paraffin wax and label. Let the sauce mature for a month before opening. Refrigerate after opening. Makes 8 cups.

Baked Tomato Sauce

I only discovered this sauce recently and I highly recommend it. It tastes very fresh and will last 10 days in the refrigerator.

> 2 kg (4 lb) tomatoes
> 1 tablespoon salt
> 1 tablespoon sugar
> 1 cup (9 fl oz) chilli vinegar
>   (page 17)
> 1 tablespoon ground ginger
> 1 tablespoon finely chopped
>   marjoram

Put the tomatoes into several baking trays and bake in a preheated oven 180°C (350°F) for an hour or until they are soft. Skin the tomatoes and put them through the food processor. Put into a pan along with the salt, sugar, vinegar, ginger and marjoram. Cook in a pan for about an hour or until the sauce has thickened. Ladle into warm, sterilised jars. Makes 4 cups.

Variation: For a pasta sauce for six people take 2 cups Baked Tomato Sauce, 1 tablespoon olive oil, add 1 tablespoon capers and 10 black olives, finely chopped. Garnish with fresh marjoram.

Chicken with Tomatoes and Black Olives

A fast way to cook chicken if you already have the sauce in the refrigerator. It looks beautiful too with the contrast of the rich red sauce and the black olives.

2 breasts or 2 thighs of chicken
Flour for dusting
1 tablespoon olive oil
4 small onions, peeled
1¹/₂ cups (13 fl oz) white wine
1¹/₂ cups (13 fl oz) Baked Tomato
   Sauce (opposite page)
1 teaspoon pepper
¹/₂ cup (3 oz) black olives, pitted

Cut the breasts or thighs in half and remove the skin and fat. Dust with flour. Put the oil in the pan and when hot, brown the chicken pieces along with the onions. Pour in the wine and tomato sauce. Stir gently and add the pepper. When the sauce is bubbling, turn the heat to a simmer and cover. Cook gently for half an hour or until tender. Put the olives in 5 minutes before serving. Serves 2.

Duxelles

This is a concentrated mushroom paste which can be used for flavouring soups, casseroles and terrines. It should last for months correctly bottled. It can also be turned into a delicious sauce by adding a quantity to Brown Sauce (page 29) or simply heating it with ¹/₂ cup wine and ¹/₄ cup cream. Keep refrigerated.

¹/₂ kg (1 lb) mushrooms
1 onion, finely chopped
3 tablespoons oil
2 tablespoons finely chopped parsley
Salt and pepper
¹/₂ teaspoon ground nutmeg

Wipe the mushrooms and chop finely. Simmer the onion in the oil until translucent, then add the mushrooms, parsley and spices. Simmer until the liquid has evaporated. Stir towards the end in case it burns. Spoon into warm, sterilised jars, press down well and pour a little oil over the surface to seal the paste. Makes 1 cup.

Horseradish

Horseradish can be used as a basis to make a variety of sauces, as it seems to harmonise with so many foods—roast beef, ham, tongue and lamb, even fish and shellfish. Try it with melted butter over boiled potatoes and broccoli. If you cannot make your own horseradish sauce, buy some and flavour it as shown in the variations.

Preserved Horseradish Sauce

The fumes from the horseradish are very intense so be careful—especially of your eyes—while preparing the sauce. If you peel it under water, you can avoid the fumes.

¹/₂ cup (2 oz) fresh horseradish,
   peeled
3 tablespoons white wine vinegar
¹/₂ teaspoon salt

Grate the horseradish in the food processor. Add the vinegar a spoonful at a time until you get the desired consistency. Mix in the salt and store in a jar. Keep refrigerated. Makes ¹/₂ cup.

Red Horseradish
Add 2 tablespoons of grated cooked beetroot to the basic sauce. It makes a beautiful colour and adds natural sweetness.

Creamed Horseradish Sauce

Use this for a dip as well as a sauce.

1 cup (9 fl oz) light sour cream or
   yoghurt
3 spring onions
2 tablespoons Preserved Horseradish
   Sauce
Pepper to taste

Mix all the ingredients together and serve immediately. Add a few drops of Tabasco for a change, or 2 tablespoons of capers.

Horseradish and Apple Sauce

Add a grated apple and 3 tablespoons of light sour cream to the basic mixture. Good with veal, pork and ham. Two tablespoons of chopped walnuts, added as well, make a piquant sauce.

Horseradish Mustard

Add 3 tablespoons of Dijon mustard to 3 tablespoons of basic recipe. Use as a sauce for fish and meat or as a marinade.

Anchovies

Buy very fresh anchovies at the markets. Wipe them clean and lay them down in a wide-mouthed jar between layers of sea salt and a sprinkle of pepper and thyme. They will keep for months in the refrigerator.

Anchovy Paste

Use this delicious paste as a sauce with strong-tasting fish, beef or pork or as a dip with crudités.

250 g (8 oz) salted anchovies or
   125 g (4 oz) tinned anchovy
   fillets
3 garlic cloves
$1^1/_2$ tablespoons white wine vinegar
3 tablespoons olive oil
Pepper

If you are using salted anchovies, split them and remove the spine. Wash well. Separate the fillets and soak in milk for 2 hours. If you are using tinned anchovy fillets, drain them of oil. Blend the anchovies and garlic in the food processor and gradually add the vinegar and oil. Season with pepper. Store in a screw-top jar in the refrigerator. Makes $^3/_4$ cup.

Anchovy Pasta Sauce

Add 3 tablespoons parsley and a chopped red chilli to half of the above recipe to serve four people. You could also add 2 tablespoons capers. Warm up to serve over pasta.

Garlic Sauce

Use this garlic sauce for making up your Asian curries and stir-fries or use as a sauce. It will last up to two months in the refrigerator.

3 tablespoons finely chopped garlic
2 red chillies, finely chopped
1 teaspoon sugar
$^1/_2$ cup (4 fl oz) white wine vinegar
1 cup (9 fl oz) water
Salt to taste, optional

Put all the ingredients into a pan and simmer slowly until the sauce is reduced and is thick and smooth. Makes $^3/_4$ cup.

Homemade Anchovy Paste (this page), to be used as a dip for crudités or as the basis of a pasta sauce. Freshly made tagliatelle lies ready in the background. All the ingredients are within reach in the pantry, so you can make a meal when the refrigerator is bare.

Chilli Sauce

This is an extra-hot chilli sauce. If you want it milder, discard the seeds when chopping the chilli. Split the chilli in half lengthwise and scrape the seeds out. Be careful not to touch your eyes while handling cut chillies.

> 250 g (8 oz) fresh chillies, chopped
> 2 onions, finely chopped
> 1 apple, peeled and finely chopped
> 1 tablespoon finely grated ginger
> 1 teaspoon salt
> 1 cup (9 fl oz) white wine vinegar

Put all the ingredients into a pan and heat gently until it boils. Simmer until the sauce is soft and thick. Blend in the food processor and pour into warm, sterilised bottles. Makes about 2 cups.

Worcestershire Sauce

Try homemade for a change. You'll be amazed at the difference. And it's so fast to make if you already have garlic sauce, anchovy paste and chilli sauce in the pantry.

> 1 litre (1³/₄ pts) malt vinegar
> 1 onion, finely chopped
> ¹/₂ cup (2 oz) ground walnuts
> 2 teaspoons Garlic Sauce (page 36)
> 3 tablespoons Anchovy Paste (page 36)
> 2 teaspoons Chilli Sauce (this page)
> 3 tablespoons light soy sauce
> 2 teaspoons pepper/salt, optional

Place all the ingredients in a large jar and seal. Shake the contents a few times a day for 2 weeks. Strain the sauce into warm, sterilised bottles and seal. Makes 1 litre (1³/₄ pts).

Green Sauce

This delicious herbed sauce is a great favourite in Italy and France. Serve it with hearty dishes such as corned beef, poached chicken or tongue. Frankly I think it tastes great with most meats, fish and vegetables. Use is as a pasta sauce as well. It will only last about 5 days in the refrigerator; however, most of the ingredients are likely to be in your pantry. It can be frozen, but it tastes much better freshly made.

> 1 cup parsley
> 2 tablespoons capers
> 1 tablespoon chopped garlic
> 2 tablespoons Anchovy Paste
>   (page 36)
> 1 small boiled potato
> Salt, optional
> 1 tablespoon wine vinegar
> ¹/₂ cup (4 fl oz) virgin olive oil
> 1 teaspoon pepper

Put all the ingredients into the food processor and blend. Gradually add the oil until it is a fairly thick, smooth sauce. Serves 6.
Variation: Use ¹/₂ cup basil and ¹/₂ cup parsley instead of 1 cup parsley.

Pesto

As well as being the great favourite pasta sauce, this rich aromatic blend will also harmonise with many meats, fish and vegetables. Use it as a dip with crudités or to garnish a soup. If you want to freeze pesto, freeze it before adding the pine nuts and cheese.

> 2 cups basil leaves
> ¹/₂ cup (4 fl oz) virgin olive oil
> 2 garlic cloves, crushed
> 2 tablespoons pine nuts
> 1 teaspoon salt, optional
> 6 tablespoons freshly grated
>   parmesan cheese
> 2 tablespoons freshly grated pecorino
>   cheese
> 2 tablespoons hot water

*P*ut all the ingredients except for the cheese into the food processor and blend. Add the cheeses gradually. Gradually add some hot water, from the pasta water preferably, until it is a smooth, thick paste. Serves 6.
Variation: If you don't have enough basil leaves, use 1 cup spinach and 1 cup basil. Substitute walnuts for the pine nuts.

Mint Sauce

Preserve mint leaves so you can eat mint sauce all through winter. Don't throw out the vinegar when you are finished. Use it for salad dressings—a dash in the gravy makes a refreshing change.

4 cups mint leaves
1½ cups (13 fl oz) white wine
    vinegar

*W*ash and dry the leaves, chop finely and pack into a warm, sterilised jar. Pour the vinegar over to cover, adding more if necessary. Seal and store in a dark cool place. Makes 3 cups. To make mint sauce for six people, take out 6 tablespoons of mint, add 1 tablespoon honey, 4 tablespoons white wine vinegar and 4 tablespoons hot water. Stir well and serve warm.

Blueberry Sauce

Use blueberry sauce to accompany poultry, pork and lamb; stir a few tablespoons into your homemade Vanilla Ice-Cream (page 160) or add to muffins if blueberries aren't in season.

2 cups (1 lb) sugar
1 cup (9 fl oz) water
Juice of 1 lemon
1.5 kg (3 lb) blueberries

*P*ut the sugar, water and lemon juice into a pan and stir until the sugar is dissolved. Bring to the boil, add the blueberries and when the liquid is boiling again cook the blueberries for 1 minute. Remove them with a slotted spoon. Turn up the heat and reduce the liquid until it has thickened. Put the blueberries into warm, sterilised jars and pour the thickened syrup over them. Seal and store.

Hot Apple Sauce

1 kg (2 lb) apples
2 onions, finely chopped
5 garlic cloves, finely chopped
1 tablespoon Chilli Sauce (page 38)
3 cups (26 fl oz) cider vinegar or
    wine vinegar
1 cup (8 oz) sugar
2 teaspoons ground cumin
2 teaspoons ground cardamom seeds
3 cloves

*P*eel, core and roughly chop the apples. Put all the ingredients into a pan, mix and bring to the boil. Simmer for about an hour or until it thickens. Stir towards the end. Allow to cool slightly, then blend it in the food processor. Put the purée back into the pan and bring to the boil. Ladle into warm, sterilised jars; seal when cool. Makes 2½ cups.

Rhubarb Sauce

10 rhubarb stalks, washed and cut
5 onions, roughly chopped
2 chillies, chopped
1 tablespoon chopped ginger
2 teaspoons pepper
2 teaspoons black mustard seeds
2 teaspoons Garam Masala
    (page 46)
1 teaspoon salt
3 cups (26 fl oz) malt vinegar
3 cups (1½ lb) sugar

Combine all the ingredients except the sugar in a pan and bring to the boil. Simmer for an hour then blend in the food processor. Put the purée back in the clean pan and add the sugar. Bring to the boil and simmer until the sauce is thick and creamy. Ladle into warm, sterilised jars, seal and store. Makes 8 cups.

Cumberland Sauce

You can make this sauce any time of the year. Try it with Seville oranges or any bitter orange for a change.

2 shallots, finely chopped
4 oranges
2 lemons
2 cups (1¼ lb) redcurrant jelly
1 tablespoon Dijon mustard
3 tablespoons red wine
½ cup (4 fl oz) port
Salt and pepper

Put the shallots in a pan, cover with cold water and bring to the boil. Simmer for a few minutes and strain. Peel oranges and lemons very thinly with a vegetable peeler; cut the peel into julienne strips. Blanch them in the same way as the shallots. Melt the redcurrant jelly in a heavy pan. Stir in the mustard, wine, port, shallots and peel. Season with the salt and pepper, simmer for about 20 minutes, until the sauce is fairly thick. It will thicken more as it cools. Bottle and keep in a cool, dark place. Makes 2 cups.

Preserve cherries so you can eat them all year round. This Cherry Sauce (this page) is a great stand-by to serve with poultry and hot or cold meats.

Cherry Sauce

I serve this sauce with my Christmas turkey and it is always very popular. It goes well with game, pork and lamb as well.

1 cup (10 oz) redcurrant jelly
1 tablespoon Dijon mustard
2 tablespoons white wine vinegar
1 teaspoon pepper
2 cups (12 oz) fresh cherries, stoned

Melt the jelly in a bowl which is placed over a pan of boiling water. Slowly stir in the mustard, vinegar and pepper until the sauce is liquid and smooth. Blanch the cherries for 5 minutes, drain and stir into the liquid sauce. Ladle into warm, sterilised jars, seal and store in the pantry. Makes 2 cups.

Plum Sauce

2 cups (12 oz) ripe plums, washed
1 cup (8 oz) sugar
A cinnamon stick
2 red chillies
3 cloves
1 cup (12 oz) redcurrant jelly
1 tablespoon port

Put the plums into the pan with the sugar, cinnamon, chillies and cloves. After the mixture comes to the boil, simmer until it is reduced to pulp. Put it through a sieve to remove the stones. Return the purée to the pan, add the redcurrant jelly and the port and bring to the boil. Simmer for a few minutes, then ladle into warm, sterilised jars, seal and store. Makes 1½ cups.

Freezer Tip: To freeze cherries, stone them and then lay them out on a baking tray to freeze. When frozen, seal in a polythene bag. Freeze mushrooms the same way.

Chinese Plum Sauce

To serve with barbecued pork or duck or with any Chinese dish that calls for plum sauce.

2 apples, peeled, cored and chopped
4 tablespoons water
500 g (1 lb) ripe red plums
1 cup (8 oz) sugar
4 tablespoons white wine vinegar
2 chillies, chopped
1 tablespoon Szechuan peppercorns

Put the apples in the pan with the water and cook until the apples are soft. Add the rest of the ingredients and bring to the boil. Simmer for about half an hour or until the mixture is reduced to a pulp. Put through a sieve to remove the stones. Ladle into warm, sterilised jars and seal. Makes 3 cups.

Prune Sauce

A quick and easy sauce to make if you have run out of pantry sauces but have a packet of prunes. Tastes good with all meats. Serve warm or cold. It will keep up to 5 days in the refrigerator.

1 cup (6 oz) stoned prunes
1 cinnamon stick
1/2 cup (4 fl oz) water
2 teaspoons butter
1 teaspoon sugar
4 tablespoons red wine

Cover the prunes and cinnamon with the water and bring to the boil. Simmer until the prunes are soft. Blend in the food processor, taking out the cinnamon first. Put the purée back in the pan with the butter and sugar. Mix well and slowly add enough wine to get a pouring consistency to the sauce. Makes 1 cup.

Mexican Orange Paste

This paste can be used to flavour poultry, lamb or pork as well as fish. It will last 10 days in the refrigerator. Otherwise freeze.

1 tablespoon chilli powder
2 teaspoons ground cumin
1 tablespoon chopped, fresh coriander
6 garlic cloves, chopped
Juice of 2 oranges
Juice of 1 lemon

Mix all the ingredients together. Store in a screw-top jar. Makes 1/2 cup.

Salsa Roja

10 red chillies, seeded
1 1/2 tablespoons tomato paste
1 garlic clove
1 tablespoon chopped, fresh coriander
2 tablespoons olive oil
1/2 teaspoon ground cumin

Pour hot water over the chillies and soak for an hour. Strain and put into the food processor along with the rest of the ingredients. Blend and then place in a pan and cook for 15 minutes or until the sauce is thick.

Spicy Powders

All cuisines have their own particular favourite combination of ground spices. Here is a collection from countries such as France, Italy, Russia, Morocco, India and China. It makes sense to have them mixed and stored ready to give an instant flavouring to terrines, sausages, casseroles and curries. They can be mixed with oil, butter, herbs, yoghurt or wine to make the base for the meats or vegetables to cook in. Experiment.

I always buy my spices whole from a reliable shop with a large turnover so they are fresh. I share with a friend and buy in bulk so my spices are cheaper. It is worthwhile investing in a food mill or coffee grinder to use as a spice mill. Nothing can compare with freshly ground spices. I keep my mixtures in the refrigerator in small sealed jars as they will keep their freshness longer. Don't hesitate to experiment if you have run out of a spice. There are usually many variations of all these powders.

Quatre-Epices

The French use this aromatic mixture to flavour sausages, pâtés and to flavour ham and pork dishes. Use it with olive oil and lemon juice to marinate barbecued meats, poultry and vegetables. A pinch in soups makes an interesting change.

    2 tablespoons peppercorns
    2 teaspoons cloves
    2 teaspoons nutmeg
    1¹/₂ teaspoons ginger

Grind all the spices in the food mill and store in a tightly sealed jar in the refrigerator. Makes 3 tablespoons.

Spezie all'Italiana

Experiment with a pinch of these spices in your pasta sauces and Italian dishes. Put it on the table as a condiment for a change.

    1 teaspoon peppercorns
    1 teaspoon cloves
    2 tablespoons ground cinnamon
    4 bay leaves, crumbled
    1 teaspoon chopped dried thyme
    3 nutmegs

Grind the peppercorns, cloves and cinnamon in the food mill. Put in a bowl and add the crumbled bay leaves and thyme. Grate the nutmeg into the bowl and mix well. Store in sealed jars in the refrigerator. Makes 5 tablespoons.

Ras el Hanout

A hot blend of spices from Morocco with many variations. Don't just use it with Middle Eastern food. Experiment with marinades, dips and mincemeat dishes as well.

    2 teaspoons peppercorns
    1 teaspoon coriander seeds
    1 teaspoon cumin seeds
    1 teaspoon cinnamon
    1 teaspoon dried rosemary
    1 teaspoon dried thyme
    ¹/₄ teaspoon cardamom seeds
    ¹/₄ teaspoon cloves
    1 teaspoon ground ginger
    ¹/₄ teaspoon grated nutmeg
    ¹/₄ teaspoon cayenne

Grind together the pepper, coriander, cumin, cinnamon, rosemary, thyme, cardamom and cloves. Add the ginger, nutmeg and cayenne and mix well. Store in sealed jars in the refrigerator.

Dukkah

This is a textured mixture of spices and nuts that is served in Egypt as an appetiser or snack. It is served with flat bread or pita bread dipped in olive oil. This is a dry spice and nut mixture, not a powdered form of spice.

    1¹/₂ cups (12 oz) coriander seeds
    1 tablespoon cumin seeds
    1 tablespoon cardamom seeds
    1 teaspoon pepper
    1 cup (8 oz) sesame seed
    ¹/₄ cup (1 oz) pine nuts
    1 teaspoon salt

Dry roast all the ingredients separately. Grind together the coriander, cumin, cardamom seeds and pepper. Add the rest of the ingredients and lightly grind them.

Cajun Spices

A fiery mixture that is used in Cajun cooking very much as you would use the first three recipes in Spicy Powders.

    1 tablespoon dried marjoram
    1 tablespoon garlic powder
    1 tablespoon paprika
    1 tablespoon ground cumin
    1 tablespoon dried thyme
    1 tablespoon onion powder
    2 teaspoons cayenne
    1 teaspoon ground pepper
    1 teaspoon salt

Mix all the ingredients together and store in a screw-top jar in the refrigerator. Makes $^1/_2$ cup.

Sri Lankan Curry Powder

This curry powder is dark roasted and has a different flavour from that of Indian powders. Use it as a flavouring to cook fish, poultry and lamb and beef curries.

    $^1/_2$ cup (4 oz) coriander seeds
    3 tablespoons cumin seeds
    2 teaspoons fennel seeds
    2 teaspoons chilli seeds
    5 fenugreek seeds
    1 teaspoon cardamom seeds
    5 whole cloves
    1 tablespoon dried curry leaves

Dry roast the coriander, cumin, fennel, chilli and fenugreek seeds separately until they each become well coloured. Grind them in the food mill. Grind the rest of the ingredients and mix well together. Choose for yourself how finely you want to grind them. I prefer to have my spices coarsely ground. Store in a small jar in the refrigerator. Makes $^3/_4$ cup.

Beef Curry

There are many ways to make up curries but the general principle is as follows. Use the curry powder as part of the flavouring. Make a paste of ginger, garlic, fresh coriander, onion and lemon juice in the blender. Add the curry powder of your choice and either water, yoghurt or coconut milk. When this is a thick luscious sauce, add the meat, chicken or vegetables. Reduce the heat to simmer, cover and cook gently for $1^1/_2$ hours.

    1 kg (2 lb) stewing beef
    1 tablespoon mustard oil
    2 large onions, finely sliced
    1 tablespoon grated ginger
    3 red chillies
    4 garlic cloves, chopped
    $^1/_2$ cup (4 oz) Sri Lankan Curry
       Powder (this page) or other
    1 teaspoon turmeric
    1 cup coriander or mint, chopped
    Juice of 1 lemon
    2 tomatoes, peeled and chopped
    1 cup (9 fl oz) Coconut Milk
       (page 25)

Trim the beef of fat and cut into bite-size cubes. Heat the oil and gently cook the onions, ginger and chillies until the onions are transparent. Add the garlic, curry powder, turmeric and coriander and cook for a few more minutes stirring all the time. Add lemon juice, tomatoes and coconut milk. Keep stirring until it is a nice thick paste. Add the meat and stir until it is all coated. Turn the heat to simmer, cover and cook for $1^1/_2$ to 2 hours. If the sauce looks too thin towards the end, take the lid off and turn the heat up until the sauce is reduced. Serves 4 to 6.

Beef Curry (this page) is simple and relatively quick if you already have a spicy powder or paste to hand. This one was made with Madrasi Masala (page 47) and I used thick Coconut Milk (page 25) as the cooking liquid. It was served with Indian Spicy Rice (page 120), and Green Tomato Chutney (page 59).

Kashmiri Curry Powder

Make a curry the same way as for the previous recipe, substituting chicken pieces for beef, yoghurt for coconut milk, saffron for turmeric and add 3 tablespoons of slivered almonds. I wouldn't add any more chilli.

$^1/_2$ cup (4 oz) cumin seeds
$^1/_4$ cup (2 oz) peppercorns
4 cinnamon sticks
$^1/_4$ cup (2 oz) cardamom seeds
$^1/_4$ cup (2 oz) cloves
$^1/_4$ cup (2 oz) chilli seeds

In a food mill grind the cumin, pepper, cinnamon, cardamom, cloves and chilli to a fine powder. Store in a jar. Makes $1^1/_2$ cups.

Panchphoran

A five-spice mixture from Bengal. The seeds remain whole and are roasted in oil just before using.

$^1/_4$ cup (2 oz) cumin seeds
$^1/_4$ cup (2 oz) black mustard seeds
2 tablespoons black cumin seeds
1 tablespoon fennel seeds
10 fenugreek seeds

Mix the seeds and store in an airtight jar. Makes $^3/_4$ cup.

Indian Spice Dip

An interesting start for an Indian meal. Prepare a plate of raw vegetables such as carrots, broccoli, beans, radishes, tiny tomatoes and fennel. Serve with a small bowl of gin and a small bowl of spice dip. Guests dip the vegetables into the gin and then into the spice mix.

$^1/_4$ cup (2 oz) coriander seeds
3 tablespoons whole cumin seeds
$^1/_3$ cup (3 oz) sesame seeds
2 teaspoons pepper
2 tablespoons salt
$^1/_2$ teaspoon chilli powder

Dry roast the coriander, cumin, sesame seeds and pepper in a small pan. When they darken they are ready. Grind the spices and add the salt and chilli. Mix well and store in an airtight jar. Makes $^3/_4$ cup.

Garam Masala

A nice big batch to make, so give some away to friends as well. Otherwise, halve the quantities. A lovely chore for a rainy day —your house will smell wonderfully aromatic. Garam masala is usually added towards the end of the cooking. You can keep some on the table as a condiment as well. Try it sprinkled on pumpkin soup or barbecued vegetables.

2 cups (1 lb) coriander seeds
1 cup (8 oz) cumin seeds
$^1/_2$ cup (4 oz) peppercorns
$^1/_4$ cup (2 oz) cardamom seeds
4 cinnamon sticks
$1^1/_2$ tablespoons cloves
5 whole nutmegs

Roast all the spices separately in a dry pan except for the nutmegs. Grind them as they cool down. Grate the nutmegs into the mixture. Put all the spices in the blender and mix well for a few seconds. Store in screw-top jars. Makes 4 cups.

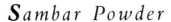

Sambar Powder

Sambars are soupy dishes made with split peas or dhal. This is powder for a very hot traditional sambar, but you can add less chilli if you prefer milder curries.

> 2 tablespoons oil
> $^1/_4$ cup (2 oz) coriander seeds
> 4 cinnamon sticks, broken up
> 10 fenugreek seeds
> $^1/_4$ cup (2 oz) dried red chillies
> 3 tablespoons chana dhal
> $^2/_3$ cup (2 oz) desiccated coconut
> $^1/_4$ cup (2 oz) dried curry leaves

Heat half the oil and add the coriander, cinnamon and fenugreek. Stir until they darken. Remove into a bowl with a slotted spoon. Now roast the chillies in the oil. Remove them to same bowl. Add the rest of oil to pan and roast the chana dhal until it turns reddish. Put in bowl. Now add the coconut and curry leaves to the pan. Stir and roast as before and put them into the bowl and mix all ingredients well together. When the spices are cool, grind them in the food mill. Put in a jar, pour a layer of oil over the top and seal well. Makes $1^1/_2$ cups.

Split Pea Sambar

Serve with vegetables and yoghurt, or have as a course on its own.

> 1 cup (6 oz) split peas or toovar
>   dhal, soaked
> 1 bay leaf
> $^1/_2$ teaspoon turmeric
> 2 tablespoons mustard oil
> 2 onions, roughly chopped
> Juice of 1 lemon
> 2 tablespoons Sambar Powder
>   (above)
> $^1/_2$ tablespoon oil
> $^1/_2$ teaspoon black mustard seeds

Wash the split peas and put them in the pan with $4^1/_2$ cups of water, the bay leaf and turmeric. Bring to the boil, cover and simmer for $1^1/_2$ hours or until cooked. Heat the mustard oil in a pan and add the onions. Cook until they are translucent. Add 2 cups of water, lemon juice and sambar powder. Stir well and bring to boil. Cover and simmer for 10 minutes. Once this is cooked, add it to the drained split peas. Put the oil in the pan and cook the mustard seeds in. Stir until they pop, and pour over the split peas. Serves 6.

Spicy Pastes and Sauces

You will find these curry pastes infinitely superior to any bought ones. When you buy and grind the spices yourself you know exactly what you are getting. Many commercial pastes bulk up the spices with ground rice and are mean with cardamom, an expensive spice. Use the pastes basically the same way as for Beef Curry (page 44). Seal the pastes in jars with a layer of oil which you can pour off every time you need some paste, then pour back again.

Madrasi Masala

> 2 cups (1 lb) coriander seeds
> 1 cup (8 oz) cumin seeds
> 2 tablespoons cardamom seeds
> 2 tablespoons pepper
> 2 tablespoons black mustard seeds
> $^1/_4$ cup (2 oz) turmeric powder
> 2 tablespoons chilli powder
> 2 tablespoons salt
> $^1/_4$ cup (2 oz) grated ginger
> $^1/_4$ cup (2 oz) crushed garlic
> $^1/_2$ cup (4 fl oz) white wine vinegar
> $1^1/_2$ cups (13 fl oz) oil

Grind together the coriander, cumin, cardamom, pepper and black mustard. Mix in a bowl along with the turmeric, chilli, salt, ginger and garlic. Add vinegar to make a thick purée. Heat oil until it is hot and begins to smoke. Turn the mixture into it and, stirring all the while, bring to the boil. Reduce the heat and simmer, still stirring, until the spices are cooked, that is, when the oil separates from the spices. Makes 4 cups.

Madras Curry Paste

A hot spicy paste. Madras curry paste is used with beef, lamb or chicken and is also wonderful for vegetable curries.

2 cups (1 lb) coriander seeds
1 cup (8 oz) cumin seeds
2 tablespoons black mustard seeds
2 tablespoons peppercorns
2 tablespoons dried chillies
1 tablespoon turmeric
$^{1}/_{4}$ cup (2 oz) crushed garlic
$^{1}/_{4}$ cup (2 oz) grated ginger
$^{1}/_{2}$ cup (4 fl oz) white wine vinegar
$1^{1}/_{4}$ cups (11 fl oz) mustard oil

Grind the coriander, cumin, mustard, pepper and chillies. Put them in a bowl and add the turmeric, garlic and ginger. Add the vinegar and stir into a thick purée. Heat the oil and add the spice mixture. Bring to the boil, stirring all the time, then turn to a simmer. Keep cooking and stirring until the oil separates from the spices. Cool and store in a screw-top jar.

An Indian vegetarian dish, Split Pea Sambar (page 47) is flavoured with hot Sambar Powder (page 47). It has a fascinating texture with the roasted chana dhal, coconut and curry leaves. Never forget the final flourish of the black mustard seeds cooked in oil until they pop.

Vindaloo Curry Paste

This is a Portuguese curry which goes very well with beef, pork or duck.

$^{1}/_{4}$ cup (2 oz) coriander seeds
6 bay leaves
1 tablespoon peppercorns
1 tablespoon cloves
2 tablespoons cardamom seeds
8 cinnamon sticks
$^{1}/_{3}$ cup (3 oz) crushed garlic
$^{1}/_{3}$ cup (3 oz) grated ginger
1 tablespoon chilli powder
3 tablespoons white wine vinegar
$^{3}/_{4}$ cup (7 fl oz) mustard oil

Dry roast the coriander, bay leaves, pepper, cloves, cardamom and cinnamon one at a time. Grind them to a powder and put in a bowl. Add the garlic, ginger and chilli. Mix together with the vinegar. Heat the oil and add the spice mixture. Cook as for Madrasi Masala (page 47). Makes 2 cups.

Beef Vindaloo

1 kg (2 lb) stewing beef
1 cup (9 fl oz) white wine vinegar
3 tablespoons vindaloo curry paste (above)
2 tablespoons mustard oil
1 onion, finely sliced
2 bay leaves

Trim the fat off the beef and cut into bite-size pieces. Marinate the meat for 24 hours in a mixture of the vinegar and curry paste. Heat the oil, add the onions and cook until translucent. Put in the meat, marinade and bay leaves. Stir until the meat is browned. Turn heat down to a simmer, cover and cook for two hours or until tender. Serves 4 to 6.

Tandoori Marinade

Use this to marinate poultry, meats and seafood. Either thread on skewers or cook large pieces whole. Grill, bake or barbecue.

1 cup (9 fl oz) yoghurt
1 onion, finely chopped
3 garlic cloves, chopped
1 tablespoon chopped ginger
$^1/_2$ teaspoon cayenne
Juice of 1 lemon
2 tablespoons Madrasi Masala (page 47)
1 tablespoon pepper
1 teaspoon turmeric

Put all the ingredients in the food processor and blend to a smooth paste. Marinate meat, poultry or seafood for at least 2 hours. While cooking, baste and turn continually.

Thai Green Curry Paste

1 tablespoon coriander seeds
2 teaspoons cumin seeds
1 tablespoon peppercorns
1 teaspoon ground ginger
$^1/_3$ cup chopped green chillies
1 onion, chopped
6 garlic cloves, crushed
1 cup chopped fresh coriander,
   including the washed root
Peel of half a lemon, chopped
1 teaspoon chopped lemon grass
1 teaspoon laos powder
1 teaspoon dried shrimp paste
1 teaspoon turmeric
1 teaspoon salt
2 tablespoons oil

Grind the coriander, cumin and peppercorns in a food mill. Put all the ingredients into a food processor and blend to a smooth paste. Spoon into sterilised jars. Cover and store in the refrigerator. Makes about 1 cup.

Thai Red Curry Paste

This paste lasts for months and saves the effort of making it whenever you feel like cooking Thai. The more dried chillies you add, the redder the paste will be; but if you remove the seeds, it is safe to increase the chillies without increasing the heat.

1 teaspoon peppercorns
2 teaspoons cardamom seeds, roasted
2 teaspoons cumin seeds, roasted
1 teaspoon ground nutmeg
1 tablespoon chopped red chillies
1 teaspoon ground ginger
2 tablespoons shrimp paste
1 teaspoon laos powder
1 onion, chopped
8 garlic cloves, chopped
$^1/_2$ cup chopped lemon grass or
   lemon peel
1 tablespoon chopped fresh coriander
   roots
Zest of 1 lemon
1 tablespoon salt
3 tablespoons oil

Grind together the peppercorns, cardamom and cumin seeds, nutmeg and chillies. Put this powder into a food processor with the remaining ingredients and blend to a smooth paste. When packing the paste into the jars, check carefully that there are no air bubbles. Store in the refrigerator. Makes approximately 2 cups.

Thai Vegetable Curry

2 cups (18 fl oz) coconut milk
2 tablespoons Green Curry Paste
   (this page)
2 potatoes, diced
1 small pumpkin, diced
2 carrots, diced
1 eggplant, diced

*B*ring the coconut milk to the boil and add the curry paste. Stir well and add the vegetables. Turn the heat to simmer and cook for 15 minutes or until tender. Do not cover. Serves 4.

Nam Prik
(Thai Chilli Sauce)

Nam Prik is one of the important Thai sauces that accompany many meals. Use it as a dipping sauce for vegetables, prawns, barbecued meats, or as a dressing for a salad or noodle dish.

- *4 tablespoons dried shrimp, chopped*
- *8 garlic cloves, chopped*
- *2 teaspoons chopped chilli*
- *2 teaspoons palm sugar or raw sugar*
- *3 tablespoons nam pla (fish sauce)*
- *4 tablespoons lemon juice*
- *2 tablespoons light soy sauce*

*P*ut the shrimp, garlic, chilli and sugar in the food processor and blend. Gradually add the nam pla, lemon and soy sauce until the sauce is smooth. Store in the refrigerator. Makes 1 cup.

Thai Marinade

A quickly prepared marinade for satay sticks, or large pieces of meat, vegetables or seafood.

- *1 teaspoon Thai Curry Paste (Red or Green, opposite page)*
- *3 garlic cloves, chopped*
- *3 tablespoons light soy sauce*
- *1 tablespoon chopped lemon grass*
- *$^1/_2$ cup (4 fl oz) Coconut Milk (page 25)*

*P*ut all the ingredients into the food processor and blend to a smooth paste. Marinate beef, pork, lamb or chicken in it for at least 2 hours. Thread onto skewers and grill, or barbecue whole.

Nuoc Cham
(Vietnamese Fish Sauce)

A dipping sauce that appears on every Vietnamese table. Use it also as a salad dressing. This version will keep for several months refrigerated. Each time you use it, add some chopped fresh chilli and garlic to the serving bowl. A mortar and pestle is far more effective for this sauce than a food processor.

- *2 fresh red chilli*
- *4 garlic cloves*
- *4 tablespoons sugar*
- *$^1/_2$ cup (4 fl oz) white wine vinegar*
- *$^1/_2$ cup (4 fl oz) water*
- *4 tablespoons lemon juice*
- *$^1/_2$ cup (4 fl oz) nuoc mam (fish sauce)*

*G*rind the chilli and garlic using a mortar and pestle. Put the sugar, vinegar and water into the pan and bring to the boil. Remove and let cool. Then add the lemon juice and nuoc mam. Stir in the chilli and garlic. Store in a screw-top jar in the refrigerator. Makes 2 cups.

Nuoc Leo (Vietnamese Peanut Sauce)

Serve with a vegetable platter or as a dip for skewered meatballs. It will last 10 days refrigerated.

- *2 tablespoons peanut oil*
- *4 garlic cloves, chopped*
- *2 fresh red chillies*
- *$^1/_2$ cup (4 fl oz) hoisin sauce*
- *$^1/_2$ cup (4 fl oz) chicken stock*
- *2 tablespoons nuoc mam (fish sauce)*
- *2 tablespoons light soy sauce*
- *$^1/_2$ cup (3 oz) dry roasted peanuts, ground*

*H*eat the oil in the pan. Add garlic and chilli. When garlic is brown, add all the other ingredients. Bring to the boil, reduce heat and simmer until the sauce is a smooth, thick texture. Store when cool in a screw-top jar. Makes about $1^1/_2$ cups.

Indonesian Curry Paste

1 cup (8 oz) coriander seeds
2 tablespoons cumin seeds
1 teaspoon cloves
2 cinnamon sticks
1 tablespoon turmeric
$^1/_4$ cup (2 oz) dried red chillies
$^1/_4$ cup (2 oz) crushed garlic
$^1/_4$ cup (2 oz) grated ginger
$^1/_2$ cup (4 oz) chopped lemon grass
Juice of 2 lemons
$^1/_2$ cup (4 fl oz) oil

*G*rind the spices in a food mill and put into the food processor. Add the rest of the ingredients except for the oil and blend together. Heat the oil and add the spice mixture. Cook until the oil separates from the spices. Cool and pack into sterilised jars. Makes about $1^3/_4$ cups.

Gulai Ajam (Indonesian Chicken Curry)

1 chicken
$1^1/_2$ tablespoons peanut oil
2 tablespoons Indonesian Curry Paste (this page)
2 cups (18 fl oz) Coconut Milk (page 25)
$^1/_4$ cup (1 oz) Coconut Butter (this page)

*C*ut the chicken into 10 pieces and trim fat off. Remove skin if you like. Heat the oil in the pan and add the curry paste. Put in the chicken pieces and brown all over. Stir in the coconut milk. Bring to the boil, stirring all the time. Add coconut butter. Cover and simmer gently for 1 hour. Serves 6.

Coconut Butter
Dry roast desiccated coconut in a pan stirring constantly. Grind it to a fine paste.

Indonesian Peanut Sauce

Peanut sauce for satay. Serve this delicious sauce with satays or to accompany vegetable crudités. You can substitute peanut butter if you haven't time to roast and grind the peanuts yourself. There is a difference in flavour, though. I like my peanuts to be crunchy and not too finely ground.

2 cups (10 oz) raw shelled and
    skinned peanuts
1 small onion, thinly sliced
2 tablespoons peanut oil
3 garlic cloves, chopped
$1^1/_2$ cups (13 fl oz) water
1 teaspoon chopped chilli
$^1/_2$ teaspoon sugar
$^1/_2$ teaspoon salt
1 tablespoon soy sauce
1 tablespoon lemon juice

*G*rind the peanuts in a food processor. Put the onion in a pan with the oil and cook until it is translucent. Add the garlic. Keep simmering and stir in

Indonesian Peanut Sauce (this page) to eat with Indonesian Lamb Satay (page 54). Marinate the meat overnight for the most tender results. Soak the sticks in water for an hour before threading so they don't burn too much.

the water, ground peanuts, chilli, sugar and salt. When the sauce is smooth, stir in the soy sauce and lemon juice. Keep refrigerated, with a layer of oil on top.

Indonesian Lamb Satay

Use this marinade for chicken, beef or pork.

1 kg (2 lb) lamb
Marinade
2 spring onions, finely sliced
3 tablespoons light soy sauce
3 garlic cloves, chopped
$1/2$ teaspoon chilli powder
Juice of 1 lemon

Cut the lamb into small pieces, discarding the fat and gristle as you go. Thread onto satay sticks. Mix the marinade ingredients together and marinate the lamb for several hours before cooking. Grill over hot charcoal and serve with peanut sauce.

Malaysian Curry Paste

Use this curry paste with coconut milk to make the basis for vegetable, chicken and pork curries. See recipe for Beef Curry on page 44. Use 2 tablespoons paste with 1 cup coconut milk for 500 g (1 lb) of meat or vegetables.

$1/2$ cup (4 oz) coriander seeds
2 tablespoons cumin seeds
2 tablespoons cardamom seeds
2 cinnamon sticks
1 tablespoon ground nutmeg
$1/4$ cup (2 oz) candlenuts or brazil nuts
Juice of 1 lemon
6 garlic cloves, crushed
2 tablespoons grated ginger
10 red chillies, chopped
1 teaspoon blachan (shrimp paste)

Dry roast the coriander, cumin, cardamom and cinnamon one at a time. Grind in the food mill and put in the food processor as they are done. Grate the nutmeg in. Add the nuts, lemon, garlic, ginger, chillies and blachan. Add enough water to make a smooth paste or blend. Store in a screw-top jar in the refrigerator. Makes 1 cup.

Chilli and Black Bean Sauce

A favourite Chinese sauce of mine. This mixture will keep up to 3 months in the refrigerator. Use it to stir-fry pork spare ribs, prawns, lamb fillets or strips of beef as well as your favourite vegetables.

4 garlic cloves
1 tablespoon chilli powder
4 tablespoons Chinese black beans, rinsed and chopped
1 tablespoon sesame oil
3 tablespoons peanut oil
1 tablespoon grated fresh ginger
1 tablespoon Szechuan peppercorns
1 spring onion, chopped
1 tablespoon rice wine or sherry

Mix the garlic, chilli and black beans together. Heat the two oils in a pan and add the ginger, pepper and spring onion. Cook for 5 minutes, remove from heat and leave to cool. Pour this over the black bean mixture and add the rice wine. Mix well, put into screw-top jar and store in the refrigerator. Garnish with extra chopped spring onions, chilli and ginger when serving. Makes $3/4$ cup.

Harissa

This is a hot paste from North Africa and really fiery. It will add zest to couscous,

stews, soups, sausages and cold meats. I mix a spoonful with yoghurt and lemon juice as a dipping sauce. I like to make my sauce thick and textured, so I don't blend it too finely.

1 tablespoon coriander seeds
1 tablespoon cumin seeds
1 tablespoon peppercorns
1 teaspoon ground cinnamon
1 cup chopped red chillies
20 garlic cloves
2 tablespoons mint leaves
3 tablespoons fresh coriander leaves
1 teaspoon salt
4 tablespoons oil

Grind the coriander and cumin seeds and peppercorns in the food mill. Then put all the ingredients in a food processor and blend to a thick paste. Keep in a sterilised screw-top jar in the refrigerator. Makes $1^1/_2$ cups.

Variation
Hot Couscous Sauce
Use this sauce to serve with couscous. The guests can pour a little over their dish according to individual tastes.

2 teaspoons harissa
2 teaspoons tomato paste
$^3/_4$ cup (7 fl oz) broth from couscous

Mix the harissa and tomato paste then slowly pour in the hot broth. Makes about 1 cup.

Chermella Sauce

There are many versions of this spicy sauce. It makes a great sauce and marinade for barbecued food. Eat it in pita bread filled with sliced barbecued lamb or meatballs. It also makes an excellent dipping sauce. It will keep for up to a week. Freeze if you want it as a stand-by.

2 onions, finely chopped
4 garlic cloves, chopped
1 tablespoon chopped red chillies
$^2/_3$ cup chopped flat-leaf parsley
$^2/_3$ cup chopped coriander leaves
1 tablespoon ground cumin
$^2/_3$ cup (6 fl oz) olive oil
Juice of two lemons

Combine all of the ingredients in the food processor. Place in a screw-top jar in the refrigerator. Makes about 2 cups.

Chicken with Olives and Chermella

Chermella sauce can be used as you would use an Indian curry paste. Serve with couscous and spicy steamed vegetables.

1 chicken
1 cup (9 fl oz) Chermella Sauce (this page)
1 cup (9 fl oz) water
1 cup (5 oz) Brined Green Olives (page 76), cracked

After washing and wiping the chicken, rub the chermella all over the outside skin, between the skin and the flesh and inside the carcase. Marinate the chicken overnight. Put the chicken in a saucepan just a bit bigger than it. Add the water, bring to the boil and simmer for half an hour. In the meantime, put the olives in a pan and cover with water. Bring slowly to the boil, drain and rinse in cold water. Add the olives to the chicken pot after the first half hour. Simmer for another 20 minutes or until the chicken is cooked. Remove the chicken to a warm oven. Reduce the sauce, and pour over the chicken to serve.

3 *Preserves of Fruit and Vegetables*

*T*he art of
preserving is extremely ancient. Our
ancestors did it to preserve food in
seasons of abundance to guard against
famine, and in the process they created
the most wonderful variations which
transform fruit and vegetables into
other equally delicious foods. Mouth-
watering delights such as spicy peach
chutney, green mango relish, bread
and butter pickles, preserved artichoke
hearts, pickled grapes, olive paste,
sun-dried tomatoes, strawberry jam,
redcurrant jelly, pineapple in rum and
raspberry liqueur. So even if we do
not need to preserve for the same
reasons these days it makes sense to
make these lovely treats yourself
because homemade is always best with
the freshest ingredients. There is also

Eggplant Preserve (page 73), Pickled Onions (page
65), Sun-Dried Tomatoes in Oil (page 88) and Preserved Artichoke Hearts (page 74) all waiting in my
pantry. You can see what a visual delight it is to
open up the doors looking for inspiration for a meal.

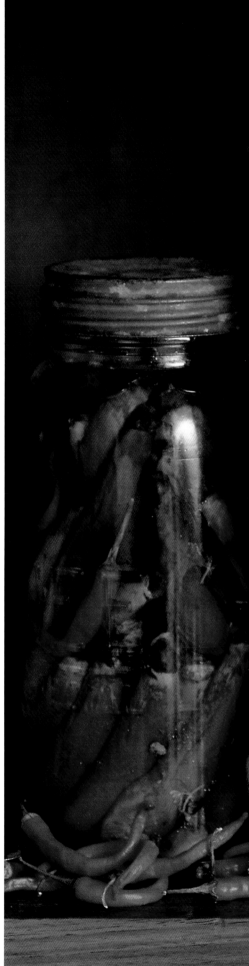

the thrill of opening your pantry door and seeing the preserves maturing and mellowing to pale yellows, mauves, greens, soft pinks and reds and the dark mysterious rows of chutneys and olives.

I have only given recipes for preserves of the simplest and foolproof kind which do not carry any preservation risk. If you are ever in doubt, throw out. Use the freshest of fruit and vegetables and transform them by preserving with oil, vinegar, salt, sugar, alcohol, spices and herbs.

Chutneys

Once chutneys were made purely to preserve the fruit but now we make them for the joy of eating aromatic blends of fruit, vinegar and sugar. They are great fun to make and don't require much expertise, so if you are a newcomer to preserving fruit and vegetables, start with the chutneys and relishes. Chutney will last for years in your pantry if by some chance you mislay a jar. They actually improve with ageing. So try to hold off eating a jar for two months after making it. The harsh vinegar taste mellows with time.

I usually use a white wine fermented vinegar but other vinegars can be used, such as malt vinegar, red wine vinegar or cider vinegar. White or brown sugar may be used. In general the darker colours will produce darker looking chutneys and the longer you cook the chutney the darker it will be. You may wrap the spices up in a muslin bag or grind them and leave them in the chutney. Always use a large heavy-based enamel or stainless steel pan that is two-thirds larger than the ingredients.

Chutney takes up to 1 or 2 hours to cook and needs to be stirred towards the end as the fruit may start sticking. You know when a chutney is ready as it becomes so thick that you can draw a wooden spoon along the bottom of the pan without any free liquid emerging. This is known as the setting point. Remove the pan from the heat and let it cool a little before ladling into sterilised jars. Use a wax disc or paraffin wax to seal the chutney if you like. Read the instructions on bottling in the first chapter before embarking on these recipes.

Lemon Chutney

A delicious accompaniment to hot curries and grills.

  1 kg (2 lb) lemons
  6 onions, chopped
  3 cups (1 lb) raisins
  10 chillies, chopped
  2 tablespoons chopped ginger
  4 cups ($1^3/_4$ lb) sugar
  1 tablespoon salt
  4 cups ($1^3/_4$ imp. pts) white wine
    vinegar

Pare the peel off the lemons and chop finely. Squeeze the lemon juice from the lemons and reserve. Put the lemon peel, onions, raisins, chillies and ginger in the food processor and blend. Mix all the ingredients together and let stand for several hours. Put into a pan and simmer until it is thick and setting point is reached. Ladle into warm, sterilised jars, cover and label. Makes about 4 cups.

Chinese Fruit Chutney

Serve with Chinese roast duck and other barbecued meats.

  1 large pineapple, peeled
  1 kg (2 lb) apricots
  1 kg (2 lb) plums
  1 tablespoon Szechuan peppercorns

750 g ($1^1/_2$ lb) sugar
1 tablespoon chopped ginger
2 cups (18 fl oz) white wine vinegar

Cut the fruits into cubes and put into a pan with the other ingredients. Simmer until the chutney is thick. Ladle into warm, sterilised bottles, seal and label. Makes 5 cups.

Apple and Mint Chutney

Perfect chutney for cold and hot lamb dishes. Also a great spread in a sandwich or pita bread.

3 apples, peeled and chopped
3 onions, chopped
1 cup mint, chopped
2 cups (18 fl oz) white wine vinegar
1 cup (7 oz) sugar
1 teaspoon black mustard seeds
3 cloves
2 chillies, chopped

Put the apples, onions, mint and vinegar into a pan. Simmer until the apple is soft then add the sugar, spices and chillies. Keep simmering until setting point is reached. Spoon into warm, sterilised jars and seal. Makes about $2^1/_2$ cups.

Quince Chutney

An unusual chutney, but full of subtle flavour. You're doing your family and friends a great favour when you decide to preserve quinces as chutneys, pastes, pickles, marmalade or even liqueur.

3 large quinces, peeled, cored and chopped
2 apples, chopped
2 onions, chopped
1 tablespoon chopped ginger

3 cups (26 fl oz) white wine vinegar
$1^1/_2$ cups (11 oz) sugar
1 cinnamon stick
3 cloves
2 chillies, chopped

Put the quinces, apples, onions and ginger in the food processor and blend. Put in a pan with the vinegar and simmer until the fruit is soft. Add the sugar, cinnamon, cloves and chillies. Simmer until the chutney is thick. Ladle into warm, sterilised bottles, seal and label. Makes about $5^1/_2$ cups.

Peach Chutney

2 kg (4 lb) yellow peaches
2 onions, chopped
1 tablespoon finely chopped ginger
2 chillies, chopped
4 cups ($1^3/_4$ imp. pts) white wine vinegar
4 cups ($1^3/_4$ lb) sugar
1 tablespoon black mustard seeds
1 tablespoon cardamom seeds

Skin the peaches by immersing them in boiling hot water for several minutes. Cut into cubes and put in the pan with all the ingredients. Simmer until the chutney is thick. Ladle into warm, sterilised bottles, seal and label. Makes about 3 cups.

Green Tomato Chutney

A firm family favourite, so much so that jars have to be hidden in unlikely places. Marries harmoniously with all cold meats and strong tasting fish. Buy a case of green tomatoes from the market. Make the chutney from some of the tomatoes, let the rest ripen for a week, then make Fresh Tomato Sauce (page 32).

2 kg (4 lb) green tomatoes, peeled
  and chopped
1 kg (2 lb) apples, chopped
500 g (1 lb) onions, chopped
5 garlic cloves, chopped
2 tablespoons chopped ginger
6 chillies, chopped
500 g (1 lb) raisins
3 tablespoons black mustard seeds
1 cinnamon stick
4 cloves
1 kg (2 lb) sugar
4 cups (1³/₄ imp. pts) white wine
  vinegar
1 tablespoon salt

Put all the ingredients into a pan.
Simmer until the sauce has thickened
to a smooth consistency and has reached
setting point. Ladle into warm, sterilised jars, cover and label. Makes 4 to
5 cups.

Relishes

Relishes are very similar to chutneys but
they don't have to cook as long because they
are generally cut much finer. They taste
fresher as a result.

Mango Relish

1 kg (2 lb) ripe mango, peeled and
  cubed
1 tablespoon chopped ginger
3 garlic cloves, chopped
¹/₂ cup (4 fl oz) vinegar
2 cups (14 oz) brown sugar
1 cinnamon stick

Put the mango, ginger, garlic and
vinegar into a pan and simmer until
mango is cooked. Add the sugar and

*Green Tomato Chutney (page 59) served with slices
of rare beef in a crusty roll—a favourite stand-by
luncheon dish.*

cinnamon. Simmer until the relish is
thick. Ladle into warm, sterilised bottles, seal and label. Makes 2 to 3 cups.

Piccalilli

*An old-fashioned favourite as a sandwich
spread with cold roast beef, lamb or ham.
You can vary the vegetables, so experiment
with what you have in hand.*

1 kg (2 lb) cauliflower florets
250 g (¹/₂ lb) pickling onions,
  skinned
250 g (¹/₂ lb) cucumbers
250 g (¹/₂ lb) apples, cored
¹/₄ cup (2 oz) salt
3 chillies, chopped
1 tablespoon chopped ginger
2 cups (14 oz) sugar
6 cups (2³/₄ imp. pts) cider vinegar
2 tablespoons English mustard
  powder
1 tablespoon turmeric
3 tablespoons cornflour

Cut the vegetables and apples into
bite-size pieces. Put them in a large
bowl, and sprinkle with salt. Cover
with a tea-towel and leave overnight.
Wash and drain the vegetables and put
them into a pan with the chillies,
ginger, sugar and 3 cups of the vinegar.
Simmer vegetables for 10 minutes and
remove from heat. Drain and pack them
into warm, sterilised jars.

Make the sauce by mixing the
mustard, turmeric and cornflour to a
smooth paste with the remaining 3 cups
of vinegar. Put it in a pan and slowly
bring to the boil, stirring all the time.
When the sauce is thick, pour it over
the vegetables, seal the jars and store.
Makes 7 cups.

Lime Relish

Makes a great sandwich spread with cold roast lamb or chicken.

4 limes
1 red capsicum, seeded and chopped
1 onion, peeled
2 celery sticks, roughly chopped
2 chillies
2 teaspoons chopped ginger
2 teaspoons black mustard seeds
1 teaspoon salt
2 tablespoons sugar
$^1/_2$ cup (4 fl oz) vinegar

Pare the zest from the limes and chop finely. Cut off and discard the pith. Cut up the lime pulp and put it with the zest, capsicum, onion, celery, chillies and ginger into the food processor. Blend and put into a pan with the rest of the ingredients. Simmer for 15 minutes. Pour into warm, sterilised jars and seal. Makes 2 cups.

Beetroot and Raisin Relish

1 kg (2 lb) cooked beetroot
500 g (1 lb) onions
250 g ($^1/_2$ lb) raisins
$^1/_2$ cup (4 oz) sugar
6 allspice berries, ground
1 teaspoon ground coriander seeds
2 teaspoons ground pepper
1 teaspoon salt
$2^1/_2$ cups (22 fl oz) white wine vinegar
$^1/_3$ cup (2 oz) flour

Roughly chop the beetroot and onion and chop them further in the food processor—do not purée, though, as the texture should be kept. Put the mixture into a pan and add the raisins, sugar, spices and enough vinegar to cover. Bring to the boil and simmer for 15 minutes. Mix the flour and the rest of the vinegar into a smooth paste. Add to the beetroot, stirring constantly until it has thickened and the flour is cooked. Pack the relish into warm, sterilised jars, cover and label. Makes about 4 cups.

Eggplant (Aubergine) Relish

A nice spicy relish. Serve with pita bread or focaccia.

1 kg (2 lb) eggplant
3 tablespoons salt
2 red capsicums, seeded
500 g (1 lb) pickling onions, peeled and quartered
3 tablespoons oil
5 chillies, chopped
3 garlic cloves, chopped
1 tablespoon chopped ginger
2 tablespoons cornflour
$1^1/_2$ cups (13 fl oz) white wine vinegar
2 tablespoons sugar
1 teaspoon turmeric
1 tablespoon ground coriander
1 tablespoon Garam Masala (page 46)

Cut the eggplant into large, bite-size pieces, sprinkle with the salt and let stand for an hour to draw out the bitter juices. Wash and dry and blanch in boiling water for 5 minutes. Cut the capsicums into large, bite-size pieces and blanch also along with the onions. Drain. Put these vegetables into a pan with the oil, chillies, cloves and ginger. Sauté for 5 minutes. Mix the cornflour with the vinegar, sugar and spices. Add to the pan and stir well until the vegetables are cooked and the sauce has thickened. If necessary, add more vinegar. Ladle into warm, sterilised jars and seal. Makes about 5 cups.

Plum Relish

2 kg (4 lb) plums, stoned and
   chopped
500 g (1 lb) onions, chopped
2 apples, peeled and chopped
4 chillies, chopped
2 tablespoons chopped ginger
3 cloves
1 teaspoon ground cardamom
1$^1/_2$ cups (11 oz) sugar
1 cup (9 fl oz) vinegar

*P*ut all the ingredients into the pan. Simmer until the volume is reduced and the relish is thick. Ladle into warm, sterilised jars and seal. Makes about 5 cups.

Shallot Sauce

An excellent sauce for barbecued chicken and beef. Shallots are not available all year round so it's sensible to make a sauce that will keep for months. Make this sauce with onions as well.

750 g (1$^1/_2$ lb) large shallots
3 tablespoons virgin olive oil
$^1/_4$ cup (2 oz) sugar
1$^1/_3$ cups (12 fl oz) red wine vinegar
$^1/_2$ teaspoon ground cinnamon
$^1/_2$ teaspoon ground nutmeg
Salt, optional

*S*oak the shallots in water for 5 minutes to make them easier to peel. Peel and thinly slice. Heat the shallots in the oil and simmer until they are translucent. Stir in the sugar, vinegar and spices and simmer until the mixture is reduced and the sauce is thick. Ladle into warm, sterilised jars and seal. Makes 2 cups.

Pickles

A good way to preserve fruit and vegetables while enhancing their flavour with salt and spices, sugar, vinegar and sometimes oil. Experiment with herb and spice combinations and different vinegars. I prefer to use a white wine vinegar but cider vinegar is interesting. I find malt vinegar too strong. Make sure your fruit and vegetables are in peak condition without blemishes. Your brine should cover the contents when bottling and leave a space of 2.5 cm (1 in.) at the top of the jar. Read about preserving in Chapter 1. Pickles are an excellent basis for making a meal in a hurry or if unexpected guests pop in. All you need is some crusty bread, one of your compound butters (page 20) and some pickled pork or cheese. A perfect alfresco meal.

Bread and Butter Pickles

2.5 kg (5 lb) cucumbers, sliced
  6 mm ($^1/_4$ in.) thick
500 g (1 lb) onions, thinly sliced
$^1/_2$ cup (4 oz) salt
Water
Ice cubes
3 to 4 cups (21 to 28 oz) sugar
5 cups (2$^1/_4$ imp. pts) white wine
   vinegar
1$^1/_2$ teaspoons celery seeds
1$^1/_2$ teaspoons black mustard seeds
1$^1/_2$ teaspoons turmeric
3 red chillies
Fennel flower sprigs

*I*n a large bowl, mix together the cucumbers, onions and salt. Cover with cold water and ice cubes and leave for 3 hours. Set aside. About 30 minutes before the cucumber mixture is ready, combine in a large saucepan the sugar, vinegar, celery and mustard seeds, tur-

meric and chillies. Stir over medium heat until the sugar is dissolved. Increase the heat and bring to the boil. Reduce the heat and simmer uncovered for 30 minutes or until very syrupy, stirring often. Drain cucumber, rinse well and drain again. Add cucumber and onions to the syrup, and heat but do not boil, stirring occasionally. Ladle the hot mixture into warm, sterilised jars when cool. Put a fennel flower sprig in each bottle. Seal. Makes about 16 cups.

Pickled Onions

A favourite pickle for young and old. I've included a recipe for a large quantity as I find they don't hang around the pantry for long once they're discovered.

2 kg (4 lb) pickling onions
1 cup (7 oz) sea salt
5 cups (2¹/₄ imp. pts) white wine
   vinegar
1 teaspoon chopped ginger
6 dried chillies
6 cloves
2 teaspoons mustard seeds
1 tablespoon peppercorns

*P*ut the onions in a bowl and pour boiling water over them. This will make them much easier to peel. Take off the roots, but leave the root end intact to ensure the onions don't fall apart. Put the onions back in the drained bowl. Sprinkle the salt over and cover with water. Leave, covered, for 24 hours. Drain and rinse thoroughly. Put the rest of the ingredients into a pan and bring to the boil. Cook for 5 minutes, remove from heat and allow to cool. Pack the onions in sterilised jars and pour the vinegar over them. Seal and label. Makes about 8 cups.

Onion sauce is made the same way as Shallot Sauce (page 63). It tastes great with cheddar cheese, rich flavoured fish, beef and poultry.

Pickled Snow Peas

This recipe works just as well with snap sugar peas.

500 g (1 lb) snow peas, string removed
1¹/₂ cups (13 fl oz) cider vinegar
¹/₂ cup (6 oz) honey
1 teaspoon coriander seeds
1 teaspoon peppercorns
1 teaspoon fennel seeds
3 red chillies

*F*ill a large bowl with water and ice cubes. Blanch the snow peas for 20 seconds and plunge straight into the iced water. Put the rest of the ingredients in a pan. Bring to the boil and remove from heat. Put the dried snow peas into warm, sterilised jars and pour the cooled liquid over the peas. Seal and label. Makes about 3 cups.

Freezer Tip: Storing Vegetables. To store vegetables for some time in the freezer, preliminary blanching is necessary to destroy the enzymes that affect the colour and flavour. Too little blanching, and the enzymes are not destroyed; too much, and you lose flavour and crispness. Blanching means dipping the vegetables into boiling water for a specified time and then immediately plunging them into iced water to prevent further cooking. Drain, and when cold, pack into polythene bags and store in freezer.

The best vegetables to freeze are: artichokes, blanch 7 minutes; broad beans and beans, 2 minutes; Brussels sprouts, 3 minutes; carrots, 3 minutes; zucchini (courgettes), 1 minute; snow peas (mange-tout), 1 minute; peas, 1 minute; sweetcorn, 6 minutes; turnips, 3 minutes; parsnips, 2 minutes; thin asparagus, 2 minutes/thick, 4 minutes; broccoli florets and cauliflower, 3 minutes; celery, 3 minutes.

Pickled Baby Beets

Small beetroots look most attractive on the plate and as part of a salad. Trim the stalk to just near the top and leave the root intact.

2 cups (18 fl oz) white wine vinegar
2 tablespoons sugar
1 teaspoon salt
10 peppercorns
1 teaspoon fennel seeds
1 teaspoon grated horseradish
   (page 36)
1¹/₂ kg (3 lb) baby beets, cooked
   and trimmed

Put the vinegar, sugar, salt, pepper, fennel and horseradish in a pan and bring to the boil. Add the beetroot and cook for 10 minutes. Let cool. Put the beets into warm, sterilised jars and pour the pickling vinegar over them. Seal and label. Makes about 3 cups.

Vietnamese Mixed Pickles

Serve these delicious pickles as a starter with rice cakes or to accompany cold pork or duck.

2 turnips, peeled and cut into sticks
2 carrots, peeled and cut into sticks
1 tablespoon salt
1¹/₂ cups (13 fl oz) nuoc mam
   (Vietnamese fish sauce)
¹/₃ cup (3 oz) sugar
2 cups (18 fl oz) water
20 shallots
20 garlic cloves
20 red chillies

Rub salt over the turnip and carrot sticks and let stand for 30 minutes. Wash and pat dry. Place them on a baking sheet and put in a preheated oven 100°C (200°F) for about 2 hours. Turn the vegetables every 30 minutes. (In Vietnam they would have been dried in the sun for a couple of days.) Remove from oven and allow to cool. Combine the rest of the ingredients in a pan and bring to the boil. Boil for two minutes, remove from heat and cool. Put the turnip and carrot sticks in sterilised jars and layer the other vegetables over the top. Pour the vinegar over, seal and label. It will be ready to eat in 10 days. Makes about 3 cups.

Pickled Chillies

Use these fiery chillies in Mexican dishes. If you can get jalapeno or serrano chillies they are the ideal variety for this.

1¹/₄ cups (11 fl oz) vinegar
¹/₂ cup (4 fl oz) vegetable oil
1 tablespoon fresh thyme
1 tablespoon ground pepper
500 g (1 lb) fresh red chillies

Combine all the ingredients except for the chillies and put in a pan. Bring to the boil and add the chillies. Boil for 2 minutes then remove from heat. When cool, spoon chillies into sterilised jars, cover with brine, seal and label. Makes 4 to 5 cups.

Pickled Turnips

Another favourite pickle in our house. This recipe is from the Middle East and is slightly different from the other pickles. It calls for a brine of salt and water as well as vinegar so the pickles tend not to last as long—only about 6 weeks. In the Middle East the leftover brine is drunk or poured over flat

Pickled Baby Beetroots (this page) make an interesting salad with black olives and mixed salad greens. Sprinkle on some virgin olive oil and balsamic vinegar.

bread. *The turnips are coloured pink with a slice of beetroot. If you can't get tiny turnips, quarter larger ones.*

$^1/_4$ cup (2 oz) salt
3 cups (26 fl oz) water
1 cup (9 fl oz) white wine vinegar
1 kg (2 lb) small white turnips, trimmed
Fennel flower sprigs
3 garlic cloves
1 small raw beetroot, sliced

Put the salt, water and vinegar in the pan and bring to the boil. Remove from heat and cool. Pack the turnips, fennel, garlic and beetroot into sterilised jars. Pour the pickling solution over, seal and label. Ready to eat in 10 days. Makes about 6 cups.

Torshi (Mixed Vegetable Pickle)

You can make up your own vegetable combination depending on what is in season. Choose from green beans, snow peas, turnips, carrots, cauliflower, cucumber, red, green or yellow capsicum (sweet pepper) and green tomatoes. Remember this will only last 4 to 6 weeks, so use vinegar if you want it to last longer.

3 kg (6 lb) mixed vegetables
8 cups (3$^1/_2$ imp. pts) water
2$^1/_2$ cups (22 fl oz) white wine vinegar
$^1/_2$ cup (4 oz) salt
1 tablespoon peppercorns
1 tablespoon fennel seeds
3 chillies, roughly chopped

Pack the vegetables into sterilised jars. Put the water, vinegar and salt together in a pan and bring to the boil. Add the peppercorns, fennel seeds and chillies and pour over the vegetables to cover. Seal and label.

Pickled Cauliflower and Red Cabbage

Another pickle from the Middle East. It will last about four weeks. Begin to eat it after a week or when it has mellowed.

1 medium cauliflower, cut into florets
$^1/_2$ red cabbage, cut into thick slices
2 or 3 chillies
4 tablespoons salt
4 cups (1$^3/_4$ imp. pts) water
1$^1/_4$ cups (11 fl oz) wine vinegar
1 tablespoon fennel seeds or flower heads

Pack the cauliflower and cabbage alternately into sterilised jars. Put a chilli and some fennel in each jar. Mix the salt, water and vinegar and pour it over the vegetables to cover. Seal and label. Makes about 7 cups.

Red Cabbage Pickle

This is ready to eat in a week, but don't leave for more than 6 weeks; it becomes soft.

1 red cabbage, finely shredded
1 cup (7 oz) salt
2$^1/_2$ cups (22 fl oz) red wine vinegar
6 juniper berries
3 bay leaves
1 cinnamon stick, crumbled

Be sure to remove the coarse outer leaves of the cabbage and the thick white stalks. Put the shredded cabbage in a large bowl, sprinkling with salt as you put it in. Cover with a tea-towel, and leave for 24 hours. Put the rest of the ingredients into a pan and bring to the boil. Keep boiling for 5 minutes, remove from heat and allow to cool. Drain and rinse the cabbage. Put into sterilised warm jars and cover with the cool pickling vinegar. Seal and label.

Pickled Green Beans

Use French beans or butter beans in peak condition. I also pickle those wonderful long, curled Italian beans that make a brief appearance in summer.

1 kg (2 lb) beans, trimmed
4 chillies
4 garlic cloves
4 fennel flower sprigs
2 teaspoons peppercorns
4 cups (1³/₄ imp. pts) white wine vinegar
1 tablespoon salt

Fill a bowl with water and ice cubes. Blanch the beans for a minute then plunge into iced water. When cool, drain and dry. Put the rest of the ingredients into a pan and bring to the boil. Keep boiling for 2 minutes and remove from heat and cool. Pack the beans, chillies, garlic, fennel and peppercorns into the sterilised jars and pour the pickling solution over. Seal and label. Makes about 7 cups.

Kim Chi (Pickled Cabbage)

Hardly a meal would go by in Korea without a dish of Kim Chi on the table.

1 white Chinese cabbage
2 cups (1 lb) sea salt
1 teaspoon chilli powder
10 spring onions, finely chopped
2 chillies, finely chopped
4 garlic cloves, finely chopped
2 tablespoons finely chopped ginger
2¹/₂ cups (22 fl oz) rice vinegar
2 tablespoons light soy sauce

Cut the cabbage into 6 segments lengthwise. Spread it on a tray and dry in the sun or in a warm place for 5 to 6 hours. Layer it in a china bowl or pot, sprinkling the salt and chilli powder over the cabbage as you pack. Cover with a wooden lid and weight it down so it compresses the cabbage. If it isn't a tight fit, put another cover over it. Keep it in a cool place for a week.

Rinse the cabbage thoroughly under running water and drain. Squeeze as much moisture out as possible. Slice the cabbage into bite-size pieces and layer it in a sterilised jar with the spring onions, chillies, garlic and ginger. Mix the rice vinegar and soy together and pour over the cabbage to cover. Seal and label. Makes 3 to 4 cups.

Green Tomato Pickle

It is definitely worth a trip to the markets to buy a case of green tomatoes. Don't just make the pickle; try the Green Tomato Chutney on page 59 too. They also make a delicious green tomato jam.

2 kg (4 lb) green tomatoes
1 cup (8 oz) salt
1 cup (8 oz) raw sugar
5 cups (2 imp. pts) white wine vinegar
3 chillies
1 tablespoon peppercorns
1 tablespoon black mustard seeds
1 tablespoon finely chopped ginger

Slice the tomatoes and put in a china bowl, sprinkling with salt, layer by layer. Leave for 12 hours. Rinse off the excess salt under a running tap and put the tomatoes into a pan with the rest of the ingredients. Bring to the boil and simmer for 5 minutes, then remove from heat. Ladle into warm, sterilised jars. Cover when cool and seal.

Pickled Gherkins

If you cannot get gherkins, buy the smallest cucumbers and slice into bite-size pieces.

1 kg (2 lb) very small gherkins
2 tablespoons salt
1 teaspoon peppercorns
2 shallots, chopped
2 cups (18 fl oz) Tarragon Vinegar
(page 17)

Place the gherkins in a bowl and sprinkle with salt. Cover and leave overnight. Wash and dry them the next day. Put the peppercorns, shallots and vinegar into a pan and bring to the boil. Remove from heat. Pack the gherkins into warm, sterilised jars and put in the shallots and peppercorns. When the vinegar is cool pour over the gherkins and seal. Makes 4 cups.

Pickled Capsicums (Sweet Peppers)

This pickle will last for 6 to 8 weeks. It will be ready to eat in a week.

1 kg (2 lb) capsicums
3 garlic cloves
1 tablespoon peppercorns
4 tablespoons salt
4 cups (1³/₄ imp. pts) water
1¹/₄ cups (11 fl oz) white wine
vinegar

Cut and seed the capsicums and cut into bite-size pieces. Pack them into sterilised jars with the garlic and peppercorns. Mix the salt, water and vinegar together and pour over the capsicums to cover. Seal and label.

Pickled Gherkins (this page) being prepared for bottling. If you cannot buy gherkins, use Lebanese cucumbers, as here, and slice into bite-size pieces. Fennel grows wild, so pick plenty when it is flowering to use for the rest of the year.

English Pickled Walnuts

If you are lucky enough to have a walnut tree or access to one, you will be able to make these delectable pickles. I love them in a hearty beef casserole added 15 minutes before the end of cooking and served with creamy mashed potatoes. Remember that the walnuts must be green and soft.

100 walnuts
2 kg (4 lb) salt
8 cups (3¹/₂ imp. pts) water
4 cups (1³/₄ imp. pts) vinegar
1 tablespoon peppercorns
2 teaspoons allspice berries
1 tablespoon finely chopped ginger

Prick the walnuts all over with a fork. Mix the salt and water together to make the brine. Pour enough over the walnuts to cover them. Reserve the brine. Soak the walnuts for 9 days, changing the brine every third day. Make up more brine if necessary. Drain off the brine and put the walnuts on a rack in the sun for 2 or 3 days until they are black.

Pack the walnuts into hot, sterilised jars. Mix together the vinegar and spices and bring to the boil. Pour over the walnuts to cover. Seal when cool and label. Ready to eat in a month and will keep for a few years.

Pickled Eggs

Another traditional English pickle to serve with cheese, pickled onions and crusty bread for lunch or to accompany cold meats.

12 eggs
5 cups (2 imp. pts) cider vinegar
1 teaspoon fennel seeds
1 teaspoon black mustard seeds
1 teaspoon peppercorns

*P*ut the eggs into cold water and bring to the boil. Let the water simmer for 10 minutes and take off heat. When water is cool, drain the eggs, rinse in cold water and shell them. Put the eggs into a sterilised jar. Mix the vinegar and spices together and bring to the boil. When it has cooled down, pour over the eggs to cover. Seal and label. Leave for 2 weeks to mellow before eating.

Cauliflower and Bean Pickle

1 kg (2 lb) cauliflower florets
1 kg (2 lb) green beans
1 cup (8 oz) salt
1 tablespoon finely chopped ginger
1 teaspoon cayenne
5 cups (2 imp. pts) white wine
vinegar

*P*ut the cauliflower and beans into separate bowls, sprinkling with salt as you layer. Leave to stand for 12 hours. Wash the salt off under running water and drain. Pour boiling water over the vegetables and drain. Pack them with the ginger into warm, sterilised jars. Mix the cayenne and vinegar together and pour over the vegetables to cover. When cool, label and seal.

Pickled Vegetables in Oil

*T*hese preserves are so expensive to buy and are usually considered luxuries. See how easy and delicious they are to make yourself with quality ingredients. I tend to use a good quality cold-pressed virgin olive oil as you can reuse the oil when the jar is finished for another batch of vegetables or use the oil for cooking and salads. The oil imparts a very rich flavour to the vegetables. Serve with plenty of bread to mop up the oil.

Fiery Chillies in Oil

Use these chillies (hot red peppers) instead of dried chillies in stews and pasta sauces. The oil itself is also useful to sprinkle over pizzas or to use as the base of a pasta sauce, with finely chopped garlic and parsley.

1 cup red chillies
2 tablespoons salt
Cold-pressed olive oil

*R*emove the stems and split chillies down one side to remove the seeds. Cut them crosswise into open rings. Sprinkle with salt as you put them into a sterilised bowl. Put a sterilised jar full of water on top of the chillies to press them down and force out the natural liquid. Leave for 24 hours.

Dry the chillies and put them into a sterilised jar and pour the oil over to cover. Seal and label. Ready in a week.

Mixed Vegetables

Choose your vegetable mixture from any of the following: eggplant, red, yellow or green capsicum (sweet pepper), zucchini (courgettes), cauliflower, onions, cucumber, green beans and mushrooms.

7 cups (3 imp. pts) wine vinegar
2 tablespoons honey
1 cinnamon stick
1 tablespoon black mustard seeds
1 tablespoon coriander seeds
1 tablespoon peppercorns
2 chillies
1 kg (2 lb) mixed vegetables, cut
into bite-size pieces
Cold-pressed olive oil
3 bay leaves
3 garlic cloves

*P*ut the vinegar, honey and spices into a pan and bring to the boil. After 15 minutes, remove from heat. Pack the vegetables into 3 sterilised jars. When the vinegar is cool, pour it over the vegetables to cover. Seal. Let the vegetables marinate for up to 9 days in the vinegar. Remove the vegetables, rinse, drain and wipe dry. Return them to the jars which have been washed and sterilised. Pour the olive oil over to cover and add a bay leaf and garlic clove to each jar. Seal and leave a week before eating.

R oasted   Capsicum (Pepper)   in   Oil

750 g (3 lb) capsicums
2 tablespoons coriander seeds
4 cloves
1 tablespoon peppercorns
6 garlic cloves
6 bay leaves
2 to 3 cups (18 to 26 fl oz) virgin olive oil

*R*oast the capsicum until the skin slips off easily. Discard the stalk and seeds and cut the capsicum into thick slices. Pack into sterilised jars along with the spices. Pour olive oil over and seal. Makes 3 to 4 cups.

W hole   Roast   Garlic in   Oil

This is so delicious to accompany a meal of cold meat and salad. Serve each guest with one whole bulb. The roasting reduces the pungency and yes, your best friends will still speak to you. You can also add individual cloves to a mixed salad.

750 g (1$^1/_2$ lb) whole garlic bulbs
3 to 4 cups (26 to 35 imp. pts) olive oil

*P*ut the garlic on a greased baking tray and put into a preheated oven 150°C (300°F) for an hour or until the cloves are tender. Remove and allow to cool. Pack the bulbs into large sterilised jars and pour oil over to cover. Seal and label.

P reserved   Basil   in   Oil

This is a sensible way to preserve a large crop of basil at the end of summer. You can use the purée to make Pesto (page 38) or as a flavouring in soups, salad dressings and over warm vegetables.

6 cups basil leaves
1 tablespoon salt
1$^1/_2$ cups (13 fl oz) virgin olive oil

*P*ut the basil, salt and 1 cup of oil into the food processor and blend, but not too finely. Put the purée into small sterilised jars, about the size of a serving. Use the rest of the oil to cover the purée and seal the contents. Put on the lid. After opening, pour another oil seal over. Makes about 2$^1/_2$ cups.

E ggplant   Preserve

This is best made with the tiny, thin eggplants that look like fingers. Use the eggplants to add to mixed barbecued vegetables or eat cold with slices of ham or cheese and tomato. A dash of Preserved Basil in Oil (this page) would be delightful.

1 kg (2 lb) baby eggplants
$^1/_4$ cup (2 oz) salt
6 garlic cloves
6 red chillies
1 tablespoon peppercorns
6 sprigs of rosemary
2 tablespoons white wine vinegar
4 cups (1$^3/_4$ imp. pts) virgin olive oil

Slice the eggplant lengthwise and sprinkle with salt. Cover and leave for 24 hours. Drain and dry and put into sterilised jars with the garlic, chillies, pepper and rosemary. Mix the vinegar and oil and pour over to cover the eggplant well. Seal and store. Makes about 10 cups.

Marinated Mushrooms

Use button mushrooms whole if they are small or quartered if large. These make a great Italian antipasto to serve with ham and salami.

> 1 tablespoon salt
> $^1/_2$ cup (4 fl oz) white wine vinegar
> 500 g (1 lb) mushrooms, trimmed
> Sprigs of oregano
> 3 bay leaves
> 3 garlic cloves
> 1 tablespoon peppercorns
> About 2 cups (18 fl oz) virgin
>   olive oil

Bring 4 cups of water to the boil and add the salt and vinegar. Put the mushrooms in the boiling water and cook for 10 minutes. Drain. Pack the mushrooms into sterilised jars along with the oregano, bay leaves, garlic and pepper. Pour the oil over and cover the mushrooms. Seal. Ready to eat in a few days. Makes about 5 cups.

Preserved Artichoke Hearts

Another Italian antipasto vegetable. Artichokes are definitely worth preserving this homemade way—so superior to any commercial ones. Eat with prosciutto and crusty bread and perhaps some Sun-Dried Tomatoes in Oil (page 88) or Pickled Onions (page 65).

> Juice of 2 lemons
> 9 medium artichokes
> 2 cups (18 fl oz) red wine vinegar
> 2 tablespoons salt
> $^1/_2$ cup (5 oz) honey
> 1 tablespoon coriander seeds
> 3 bay leaves
> 3 to 4 cups (26 to 35 fl oz) virgin
>   olive oil

Put the lemon juice in a bowl of water ready to put the artichokes in as soon as they are cut so they won't discolour. With scissors, remove the tough outside leaves and trim the tips of the leaves. Cut the artichokes vertically into six wedges. Now remove the hairy choke (centre, or heart). Put the 3 cups water into a large pan with the red wine vinegar and bring to the boil. Add salt, honey and the artichokes. Bring to the boil again quickly and cook for 8 minutes. Drain the artichokes, cool and dry. Pack the artichokes into sterilised jars along with the coriander and bay leaves. Pour the oil over to cover and seal. Ready to eat in a few days. Makes about 7 cups.

Freezer Tip: Tomatoes. Frozen tomatoes can never be used as salad vegetables because of their high water content. It make sense to purée them or freeze them skinned and chopped when you don't have time to make a sauce. In this state, they are ready for a sauce or a soup—just take out some chicken stock, a bouquet garni and some tomato pulp and there you have a hot or chilled soup. Garnish with fresh basil or some frozen pesto.

Marinated Mushrooms (this page) ready to toss through a salad or serve as an antipasto dish. If you can find the wild field mushrooms, they taste even better—try to resist eating them immediately.

Olives

Olives are very useful to have on hand for a snack, to flavour a casserole or to add that extra dash to an impromptu meal. It's fun to brine them yourself—if you haven't time, buy the brined olives in the supermarket and simply marinate them yourself with some of these ideas. They taste better than those expensive jars you buy and they'll please your purse even more. Keep the oil left in the jar for cooking or for marinating another batch.

Brined Green Olives

Green olives are very bitter, so they must be cured to make them milder before they are put in the brine. For brining black olives just omit the first step of curing them. The olives are ready to eat in 3 weeks, though they will get milder the longer they remain in the brine. If they begin to ferment, change the brine.

> 1.5 kg (3 lb) green olives
> 1 cup (7 oz) salt
> 5 litres (9 imp. pts) water
> Rind of a lemon
> 2 tablespoons rosemary
> 3 bay leaves
> 2 heads of Whole Roast Garlic in
>   Oil (page 73)

Make sure all the green olives are sound and wash them. Squash them gently with a rolling pin so that the flesh cracks but the olive remains whole. Soak the olives in water in a china bowl for eight days, changing the water every second day. Drain the olives. Make the brine with the salt and water in a large jar and put in the green or black olives. Add the orange peel, herbs and garlic, peeled, to the brine. Cover.

Marinated Green Olives

Green olives go really well with Marinated Fresh Cheese (page 147), fresh crusty bread and tomatoes—and that is lunch!

> 500 g (1 lb) brined olives, drained
> 1/2 cup flat-leaf parsley and
>   coriander, chopped
> 2 garlic cloves, chopped
> 2 teaspoons Harissa (page 54)
> Olive oil to cover

Pack the olives into sterilised jars, sprinkling the herbs, garlic and harissa in as you go. Cover with olive oil and seal.

Variations:

Moroccan Olives
Add some chopped Preserved Lemon (page 79) to the marinade above.

Herbed Olives
To 500 g (1 lb) olives add 1/3 cup thyme, 6 garlic cloves and 10 crumbled bay leaves.

Stuffed Green Olives

> 2 cups (10 oz) large, Brined Green
>   Olives (this page)
> 1/2 cup (2 oz) ground almonds
> 1 tablespoon finely chopped parsley
> 1 teaspoon ground pepper
> About 1 cup (9 fl oz) virgin olive oil
> 1 tablespoon white wine vinegar
> 1 tablespoon oil

Pit the olives. Mix all the other ingredients together and stuff the olives with the mixture. Pack into sterilised jars and cover with oil.

Green Olive Paste

Use this same recipe for black olives and omit the ground almonds and it is known as tapénade. They are both eaten as tapas and dips and to spread on crusty bread as a starter. Makes a good sauce for pasta, meats and vegetables.

> 40 green olives, stoned
> 1 tablespoon chopped capers
> 2 anchovies, mashed
> 1 teaspoon ground almonds
> 2 garlic cloves
> 1 teaspoon ground pepper
> 2 tablespoons olive oil
> Juice of $^1/_2$ lemon
> 1 tablespoon virgin olive oil

Put all the ingredients in the food processor and blend to a fine paste. Add more oil if necessary. Pack into sterilised jars and seal with a layer of oil. Makes 1 to 2 cups.

Black Olives with Lime and Chilli

> 2 cups (10 oz) brined black olives
> Zest of 2 limes
> 10 chillies
> 2 garlic cloves
> Olive oil to cover

Drain the olives and put into jars with the lime zest, chillies and garlic. Cover with oil and seal.
Variations:

Black Olives with Harissa
Mix brined olives with Harissa (page 54) and sprinkle a little oil over just before serving for a quickly prepared marinade. Bottle it in oil this way as well.

Marinated Black Olives
For 500 g (1 lb) olives, make a marinade of 2 tablespoons red wine vinegar, 2 garlic cloves, 1 tablespoon paprika, $^1/_2$ orange, sliced and chopped and $^1/_3$ cup olive oil.

Herbed Olives
For 500 g (1 lb) olives add 6 twigs of rosemary, thyme and oregano, 2 garlic cloves, 1 tablespoon peppercorns and olive oil to cover.

Pâte d'Olives (Black Olive Paste)

Use olive paste to spread on Pizzas (page 149), crusty bread or toast, add to Mayonnaise (page 31) or as a sauce with duck and chicken. This is a lesser known version of tapénade. It depends more on the olive flavour, so use fine tasting olives.

> 2 cups (10 oz) black olives, stoned
> 1 teaspoon chopped fresh thyme
> 4 juniper berries, crushed
> 1 small onion, chopped
> 3 garlic cloves, chopped
> 2 tablespoons olive oil

Put all the ingredients into the food processor and blend to a smooth paste, adding more oil if necessary. Pack into sterilised jars and cover with a layer of oil to seal. Keep refrigerated. It should last at least 3 weeks. Makes about $1^1/_2$ cups.

Freezer Tip: Cheese. Hard cheese freezes well in a large wedge—cheeses such as cheddar, edam, gruyère, parmigiano-reggiano, pecorino, colby, double, Gloucester, Swiss and gouda. Grated cheese remains free-flowing when frozen and will keep fresher frozen.

Pickled Fruit

Preserved Lemons

Lemons are preserved in Morocco and used chopped in salad or as a flavouring for chicken and meat dishes.

> 10 lemons
> 500 g (1 lb) salt
> 2 bay leaves, crumbled
> 1 cinnamon stick, crumbled
> $^1/_2$ cup (4 fl oz) lemon juice

Quarter the lemons lengthwise, leaving the last piece uncut so the lemon pieces remain attached. Stuff them with salt. Put a layer of salt in the bottom of a large sterilised jar. Pack the lemons, bay leaves and cinnamon into the jar sprinkling with the rest of the salt as you go. The lemons should be pressed down hard on top of each other. Pour in the lemon juice and seal. The salt will release the juices from the lemon and you will have them soaking in a brine. Shake the jar from time to time. They will be ready in 4 weeks.

Pickled Cherries

> 1 kg (2 lb) cherries
> 4 cloves
> 1 cinnamon stick
> 1 teaspoon ground nutmeg
> 1 teaspoon thyme
> 4 cups ($1^3/_4$ imp. pts) Tarragon
>   Vinegar (page 17)
> $^1/_2$ cup (4 oz) sugar

Wash and dry the cherries and cut off half the stalk. Put the rest of the in-

The preparation for making pickled peaches. Follow the recipe for Honey-Spiced Apricots (page 79) to make this splendid preserve. Use sugar or honey, vary the spices or leave the spices out if you prefer.

gredients into a pan and bring to the boil. Add the cherries for 2 minutes and remove them. Pack the cherries into sterilised jars and when the vinegar is cool, pour over and cover. Seal and label. Makes about 8 cups.

Honey-Spiced Apricots

Peaches also taste wonderful preserved this way. These pickles go extra well with turkey, duck and goose.

> 1 cup (11 oz) honey
> $1^1/_2$ cups (13 fl oz) white wine
>   vinegar
> 4 cloves
> 8 cardamom pods
> 1 teaspoon peppercorns
> 1.5 kg (3 lb) apricots

Put all the ingredients except the apricots into the pan. Bring to the boil and simmer for 15 minutes. Add the apricots for about 5 minutes—don't overcook them. Pack the apricots into warm, sterilised jars. Pour the syrup over them, seal and label. Makes 5 cups.

Pickled Oranges

Serve this with ham, pork, chicken or Duck Terrine (page 133). Or cut into small pieces to go in a watercress or spinach salad. A few black olives (page 76) would go well and there you have a splendid lunch.

> 8 oranges
> 1 cup (11 oz) honey
> 1 cup (9 fl oz) white wine vinegar
> 1 cinnamon stick
> 4 cloves
> 8 cardamom pods
> 3 star anise

Do not peel the oranges but discard the two ends. Slice all the oranges

and put into a pan. Cover with water and simmer until the orange is nearly cooked. Remove from heat. At the same time put the honey in a pan with the vinegar and spices. Bring to the boil and remove from heat. Pack the oranges and spices into warm, sterilised jars and pour the vinegar over to cover. Seal and label. Makes about 7 cups.

Pickled Pears

These pears go well with cold corned beef and ham. With prosciutto it makes a lovely starter to a meal with a few mesclun leaves.

> 1 cup (9 fl oz) water
> 1 cup (11 oz) honey
> 1¹/₂ cups (13 fl oz) cider vinegar
> 1 cinnamon stick
> 6 cloves
> 1 bay leaf
> 1 teaspoon peppercorns
> 8 ripe but firm pears, peeled, cored
>   and quartered

*P*ut all the ingredients except the pears in a pan. Bring to the boil and put in the pears. Simmer until the pears are cooked and translucent—do not over-cook. Pack the pears into warm, ster-ilised jars with the spices. Reduce the syrup by ¹/₃ and pour over the pears. Seal and label. Makes about 6 cups.

Pickled Grapes

Use this recipe for pickling plums as well.

> 500 g (1 lb) firm seedless grapes
> ¹/₃ cup (3 oz) sugar
> 1 teaspoon salt
> 1 cup (9 fl oz) white wine vinegar
> ¹/₂ cup (4 fl oz) water
> Zest of 1 lemon
> 4 cloves
> 1 cinnamon stick

*P*ack the grapes into sterilised jars. Place the rest of the ingredients in a pan and bring to the boil. Simmer for 15 minutes then allow to cool. Pour over the grapes and seal. Makes about 4 cups.

Pickled Cumquats

Serve this delectable pickle with chicken, duck and pork. Or add some to a watercress or mesclun salad with some of the juice as part of the dressing.

> 500 g (1 lb) cumquats
> 1 cup (8 oz) sugar
> 1 cup (9 fl oz) white wine vinegar
> 1 teaspoon cumin seeds
> 1 cinnamon stick
> 1 teaspoon peppercorns

*P*ut the cumquats into a pan and cover well with water. Bring to the boil and reduce to a simmer until the cumquats are tender. Remove from the heat. In the meantime, put the sugar, vinegar and spices into a pan, stir until sugar is dissolved and bring to the boil. Remove from heat.

Drain the cumquats into a pan. Pour the sugar-vinegar syrup over the fruit. Put on the heat and simmer until the cumquats look a bit transparent and candied. Put the fruit into a warm, sterilised bottle and pour the syrup over to cover. Seal when cool. Leave 3 to 4 weeks to mature.

Pickled Plums

These plums go well with hot or cold meats and poultry and are wonderful to eat in the depths of winter as a reminder of sunnier times.

> 1 kg (2 lb) plums, stalks removed
> 2 cups (10 oz) brown sugar
> 3 cups (26 fl oz) red wine vinegar
> 1 cinnamon stick
> 3 cloves
> 1 teaspoon peppercorns
> 5 cardamom pods

Prick the plums eight times with a skewer. Assemble the rest of the ingredients in a pan and bring to the boil. Let simmer for 10 minutes. In the meantime, pack the plums into warm, sterilised jars. Allow the pickling syrup to cool a little, then pour over the plums to cover and seal.

Freezer Tip: Puréed Fruit. Wash, slice, seed, skin the fruit—whatever is necessary. Put in a pan with a little water to cover, add sugar if liked, but make a note how much is added for when re-using. When fruit is almost cooked put it through the food processor. Pack in airtight containers, label and freeze when cool. To keep the natural colour, add $1/4$ teaspoon of ascorbic acid to 500 g (1 lb) fruit. Puréed fruit will last 4 months in the freezer.

These are the fruits that make good frozen purée: avocado, apple, apricot, banana, blackberries, raspberries, strawberries, black and red currants, blueberries, plums, gooseberries, mangoes, nectarines, peaches and rhubarb. Berry fruit can simply be puréed without cooking.

Thick Spicy Pickles

Lime Pickle

A wonderful pickle to serve with curries and vegetable dishes. Good in a sandwich with cold meats as well. Add it to yoghurt to made a dip.

> 12 limes
> 6 chillies
> 1 tablespoon chopped ginger
> 2 garlic cloves, chopped
> 2 cups (18 fl oz) white wine vinegar
> 1 teaspoon salt
> 2 tablespoons Madrasi Masala
>   (page 47)

Cut each lime into 8 wedges lengthwise. Put them in the pan with all the other ingredients. Simmer until the fruit is tender and the sauce thick. Ladle into sterilised jars and seal. Makes about 3 cups.

Hot Tomato Pickle

Delicious spread on sandwiches with ham or rare beef as well as an addition to the curry table.

> 5 tablespoons mustard seed oil
> 1 tablespoon turmeric
> 2 tablespoons black mustard seeds
> 3 tablespoons ground cumin
> 3 tablespoons ground coriander
> 2 teaspoons chilli powder
> 3 tablespoons finely chopped ginger
> 2 kg (4 lb) tomatoes, peeled and
>   chopped
> 10 garlic cloves, chopped
> 10 chillies, chopped
> 1 tablespoon salt
> $1^{1}/_{2}$ cups (13 fl oz) wine vinegar

Heat the oil in a pan and add the spices. Stir for a few minutes then add the tomatoes, garlic, chilli, salt and vinegar. Simmer until the paste is thick and the oil begins to separate from the mixture. Ladle into warm, sterilised jars and seal.

Green Mango Pickle

6 green mangoes, cut into 8 pieces
20 chillies, split and seeded
1/4 cup (2 oz) salt
6 garlic cloves, chopped
2 tablespoons chopped ginger
3 tablespoons cumin seeds
3 tablespoons coriander seeds
1 tablespoon black mustard seeds
2 teaspoons turmeric
1 1/4 cups (11 fl oz) white wine vinegar
1 cup (9 fl oz) mustard oil

Sprinkle the mangoes and chillies with salt and put onto a baking tray. Put into a preheated oven 50°C (120°F) so they can dry. It will take about 6 hours but keep checking. (In India this would be done in the sun.) Put the garlic, ginger and spices and a little of the vinegar into a food processor and blend. Put the mustard oil into a pan and stir in all the ingredients. Bring to the boil and simmer until the mango is tender and the oil separates. Cool and ladle into sterilised jars and seal. Makes about 3 cups.

Fresh Cumquat Pickle

This is another version of thick spicy pickles that go wonderfully with so many snack dishes. The pickle itself can be the inspiration for accompaniments.

20 cumquats, sliced
2 cups (18 fl oz) white wine vinegar
1 teaspoon salt
3 teaspoons Madrasi Masala (page 47)
2 chillies

Put all the ingredients into pan and simmer until the cumquats are tender and the sauce is thick. Ladle into a sterilised jar and seal.

Eggplant (Aubergine) Pickle

1 kg (2 lb) eggplants (aubergines)
2 tablespoons salt
1 cup (9 fl oz) mustard seed oil
6 chillies, chopped
2 onions, chopped
6 garlic cloves
2 tablespoons chopped ginger
3 tablespoons mustard seeds
1 tablespoon ground coriander
1 tablespoon ground fennel
1/2 teaspoon chilli powder
1 teaspoon turmeric
1 1/4 cups (11 fl oz) white wine vinegar

Slice the eggplants, sprinkle with salt and leave to degorge for an hour. Wash, drain and dry them. Heat the oil in a large pan and fry them in batches until brown on each side. Reserve the oil.

Put the chillies, onions, garlic and ginger into the food processor and blend to a paste. Put the oil back into the pan and add more if necessary. Put in the spices and heat for 5 minutes, stirring often. Now add all the remaining ingredients and stir well. Bring to the boil and simmer until the eggplants are tender, the sauce has thickened and the oil begins to separate. Cool a little, pack into sterilised jars, seal and label.

Green Mango Pickle (this page) with the fresh ingredients. You actually dry the mango slices before making them into a pickle. See the lovely texture with the curry leaves and spices coarsely ground.

Pawpaw Pickle

$^1/_2$ cup black mustard seeds

3 cups (26 fl oz) white wine
    vinegar

2 tablespoons mustard oil

1 teaspoon turmeric

1 tablespoon ground coriander

1 tablespoon ground cumin

10 chillies, chopped

5 garlic cloves, chopped

2 tablespoons grated ginger

1 green pineapple, peeled and diced

1 green pawpaw (papaya), peeled
    and diced

Soak the mustard seeds in vinegar for
12 hours. Put the oil on the heat and
add the turmeric, spices, chilli, garlic
and ginger. Cook, stirring, for five
minutes then add the vinegar and mustard seeds, the pineapple and pawpaw.
Simmer until the fruits are tender and
the sauce has thickened. Ladle into
sterilised jars and seal.

Lemon Pickle

12 lemons

20 chillies

1 tablespoon cumin seeds

1 tablespoon coriander seeds

1 tablespoon black mustard seeds

10 cardamom pods

1 teaspoon fenugreek seeds

2 tablespoons curry leaves

5 tablespoons mustard seed oil

10 garlic cloves, chopped

2 tablespoon finely grated ginger

1 cup (9 fl oz) white wine vinegar

Cut the lemons into 6 wedges lengthwise and then halve crosswise. Remove
the stem of the chillies and slit down
one side to remove the seeds.

Dry roast the spices individually. As
they begin to smoke, set them aside.
Heat the oil in a large pan, and cook
the garlic and ginger for several minutes. Now add all the other ingredients.
Stir well. Bring to the boil and simmer
until it is a nice thick paste. Pour into
a warm, sterilised bottle and seal.

Drying Fruit, Vegetables and Herbs

Don't sneer at dried fruit and herbs.
Drying concentrates the flavours and, with
the addition of moistening agents such as
wine, fruit juice and oil, you can make a
virtue of dried things. Every pantry should
have a store of these delectable items whether
you dry them yourself or not. Drying is a
very ancient method of preserving food. The
principle is to remove all moisture from the
food by heat or wind, or both, thereby in-
hibiting the growth of the bacteria that cause
food to break down. I'm only suggesting
that you consider drying food that it makes
economic sense to dry or because you may
not wish to eat food with preservatives in
it. You need an oven that will give you the
low temperature of 50°C (120°F) or a place
with good ventilation. It is possible to make
excellent dried food at home with a food
dehydrator, an appliance that is now available for home use. Experiment with drying
outside too.

Apples, Apricots, Peaches, Nectarines and Pears

Make a brine solution of $^1/_4$ cup of salt
to a large bowl of water. Peel and core
the apples and cut into 6 mm ($^1/_4$ in.)
rings. Halve and stone the apricots,
peaches and nectarines. Peel, core and

Sun Dried Tomato Purée

Take out some of the tomatoes, thyme and garlic (see preceding recipe) and blend in the food processor. Use as a sauce for pizza, pasta or meat and vegetables. If you want to make enough to store, be sure to put a seal of olive oil on top of the purée in the jar.

Garlic and Onions

A friend grows and gives me fresh garlic and onions. I plait their long leaves and hang the bunches up to dry. Not only are they decorative but they are a useful addition to pantry ingredients.

Jams, Marmalades, Jellies and Conserves

A fine jam is a joy to behold. Experience the joy of opening the pantry doors and seeing jams gleaming away—all the goodness of summer in a jar. A good jam or jelly should be transparent and the colour of the original fruit. White granulated sugar or caster sugar is used as it doesn't alter the colour of the fruit. Read Chapter 1 on preserving first if you haven't made jam before.

A good set in the jam is gained when the fruit selected has the right amount of pectin and acid in it, or when a fruit with high pectin and acid is added. The fruit should be fresh and slightly underripe, as that is when it has the most pectin. The fruit needs to be cooked gently for some time in order to break down the cell walls and extract the acid.

In most cases the sugar is added after the fruit is cooked, to preserve the colour and flavour which are spoilt if the fruit and sugar are cooked together too long. Often the sugar should be warmed before adding, that is,

put into a preheated oven at 180°C (350°F) for 20 minutes.

Setting point is reached when the jam is at 110°C (220°F). You can test this with a warmed thermometer or dip a wooden spoon into the jam and turn it sideways— if the jam is partly set on the spoon and the drops break off cleanly, the setting point is reached. You can also drop a teaspoon of jam on a plate taken straight from the freezer. The jam should set and crinkle when pushed with your finger. Turn the plate upside down—if the jam doesn't fall, setting point is reached.

When the jam reaches setting point, remove from heat. Remove any scum on the surface. Allow the jam to cool in the pan for up to half an hour and stir once. This will prevent the fruit from rising to the top of the jar.

Never use a metal lid for jams and jellies. The jars can be covered with cellophane or parchment as well as screw-top lids. A seal of melted paraffin wax or wax discs can be used as an extra precaution against mould. Store in a cool, dark, airy place.

Marmalade takes longer to cook than jam—it may take up to 2 hours before the sugar is added. Pectin is found in the pips and pith of citrus fruit so when slicing the fruit remove pips and tie in a muslin bag. The bag is removed when the fruit is cooked, just before adding the sugar. Squeeze the bag over the pan as hard as possible to let the pectin drop back into the marmalade.

A good set on a jelly is a little wobbly. Be careful when bottling not to move the jars until the jelly is well set. Do not use large jars. If you don't have a jelly bag use a colander with three layers of muslin over it. Never squeeze the jelly bag or try to force the juice through the muslin as it will cloud the jelly. When the fruit pulp is strained, measure the juice by the cupful as you put it back in the pan. You need one cup of sugar for every cup of fruit juice. Test for setting point the same as for jam.

Rhubarb and Ginger Jam

2 kg (4 lb) rhubarb
Juice and zest of 2 lemons
Juice and zest of 2 oranges
5 cups (2¹/₂ lb) sugar
2 tablespoons chopped ginger

Chop the rhubarb into 3 cm (1¹/₄ in.) lengths. Put into the pan with the lemon and orange juice and zest. Bring to the boil, cover and simmer for about 10 minutes, then add the sugar and ginger. Stir constantly until it is a thick pulp. Boil rapidly until setting point is reached. Ladle into sterilised jars, cover and label.

Summer Berry Jam

This is an especially lovely jam. Delicious spread on cakes or as a base on a fruit tart too.

1 kg (2 lb) berry fruits (raspberries,
    strawberries, red and black
    currants, etc.)
Juice and zest of 1 lemon
1 kg (2 lb) sugar

Wash, stalk and hull the fruits. Put into a pan with the lemon and put on a protective mat and the lowest heat until it is simmering. Meanwhile, warm the sugar in the oven to make it dissolve more quickly so the fruits don't get overcooked. Add the sugar to the pan as the fruit begins to simmer. Remove the mat. Stir until sugar is dissolved. Bring to the boil and boil rapidly for about 10 minutes or until setting point is reached. Ladle into sterilised jars, seal and label.

Strawberry Jam

Strawberry jam is very difficult to set. Don't despair if it doesn't set—call it strawberry conserve! It tastes just as good. Use this recipe for raspberries as well.

1 kg (2 lb) strawberries, hulled
4 cups (2 lb) sugar
Juice of 2 lemons

Put a layer of strawberries into a pan and cover with some of the sugar. Continue to layer until you have run out of both. Pour the lemon juice over. Put it on the lowest heat with a protective mat and let the sugar slowly melt. Remove the protective mat and bring to the boil. Skim off any impurities. Continue to boil until setting point is reached. Ladle into sterilised jars and seal.

Blackberry Jam

We still love to go blackberrying and, although they are a noxious weed in Australia, we always know where there are plenty to pick in late summer. Make a liqueur out of them by following the recipe for Liqueur de Cassis (page 104).

1.5 kg (3 lb) blackberries, hulled
Juice and zest of 2 lemons
1 kg (2 lb) sugar

Put the blackberries and lemon into the pan. Bring to the boil slowly. Simmer for 10 minutes and add the sugar. Stir until it is dissolved, then bring to a rapid boil; cook until setting point is reached. Ladle into sterilised jars and seal.

Blackberry Jam (this page) is one of my favourite breakfast jams. Use it also as a base for fruit tarts or stir a spoonful into a cup of hot water for a refreshing drink.

Plum Jam

1 kg (2 lb) plums, halved and
  stoned
Juice and zest of 2 lemons
2 cups (1 lb) sugar

Put the plums into the pan with the lemon. Bring to the boil and simmer for 10 minutes or until the plums are soft. Add the sugar and stir until sugar is dissolved. When it has come to the boil, turn the heat up and boil rapidly until setting point is reached. Ladle into sterilised jars and seal.

Orange and Apricot Jam

500 g (1 lb) dried apricots
4 oranges
1 lemon
2 cups (1 lb) sugar
1 tablespoon brandy

Put the apricots into the pan and just cover with boiling water. Simmer. Pare the zest from the oranges and lemon with a vegetable peeler. Cut into julienne strips. Chop up the pulp devoid of the white pith. When the apricots have been simmering for 15 minutes, add the citrus and simmer for another 20 minutes. Add the warmed sugar, stir until dissolved, then bring to a rapid boil until setting point is reached. Stir in the brandy when the jam has cooled a little, ladle into sterilised jars, seal and label.

Orange Marmalade

The simplest of marmalades and the most popular. If you can get Seville oranges or bitter oranges, use them for preference.

1.5 kg (3 lb) oranges
Juice and peel of 1 lemon
9 cups (4 imp. pts) water
3 kg (6 lb) sugar

Slice the oranges finely and put the pips and the lemon peel into a muslin bag. Warm the sugar. Place the oranges, muslin bag and water in a saucepan and bring the fruit gently to the boil. When it is tender, add the sugar. Stir until the sugar is dissolved. Remove the muslin bag, squeezing the juice back into the jam. Boil rapidly for 15 to 20 minutes or until setting point is reached. Remove from heat and let rest for 20 minutes. Take off any scum and spoon the marmalade into sterilised jars. Cover, label and seal when cold.

Grapefruit and Orange Marmalade

These two citrus fruits harmonise to make an excellent marmalade. Don't just use it for breakfast. Use it to glaze some pork chops for the barbecue, or even a duck. The raw sugar will make it a darker richer colour.

2 grapefruit
2 oranges
6 cups (2$^3/_4$ imp. pts) water
1 kg (2 lb) raw sugar

Cut the grapefruit and oranges in half and squeeze out the juice. Strain the juice into a saucepan. Take some of the thick pith off the grapefruit and put it into a muslin bag with the pips. Slice the grapefruit and orange skins. Place them in the saucepan with the fruit juice; add the bag of pith and pips and the water. Bring to the boil. When the peel is soft, add the sugar, stirring until dissolved. Remove the muslin bag, squeezing the juice into the jam. Bring to a rolling boil and cook for 15 minutes or until the setting point is reached. Pour into sterilised jars. Cover, label and seal when cold.

Chunky Cumquat Marmalade

A heavenly jam to eat with game and poultry as well as breakfast toasts and breads.

> 1 kg (2 lb) cumquats
> Juice and peel of 1 lemon
> 4 cups (1³/₄ imp. pts) water
> 1 kg (2 lb) sugar

Slice the cumquats into 3 or 4 thick slices depending on their size. Remove the seeds. Put the seeds in a muslin bag. Cut the lemon peel into julienne strips. Place the cumquats, lemon juice and peel and water in a saucepan with the bag of seeds and bring to the boil. Simmer for 1¹/₂ hours or until the cumquat skins are tender. Take out the muslin bag. Squeeze the bag thoroughly, allowing the remaining pectin to fall into the jam. Add the sugar and stir until it dissolves. Bring to a rolling boil and cook for 25 minutes or until the setting point is reached. Remove from the heat and spoon into sterilised jars. Cover immediately, label and seal when cold.

Orange, Lime and Lemon Marmalade

A popular blend of three citrus fruits. Experiment with different citrus—grapefruit, lemon, lime, mandarin, tangelo, sweet and bitter oranges and cumquat.

> 500 g (1 lb) oranges
> 500 g (1 lb) limes
> 500 g (1 lb) lemons
> 9 cups (4 imp. pts) water
> 3 kg (6 lb) sugar

Slice the oranges, limes and lemons finely and put the pips into a muslin bag. Place the slices of citrus, the bag of pips and the water in a saucepan. Bring slowly to the boil and simmer for about 1¹/₂ hours or until the peel is tender. Add the sugar and stir until it is dissolved. Take out the muslin bag; squeeze it to allow the remaining pectin to return to the jam. Bring to a rolling boil and cook until setting point. Remove from the heat, ladle into sterilised jars, label and seal.

Redcurrant Jelly

A very handy jelly in the pantry and a basis for other delicacies such as Cumberland Sauce (page 41) and Cherry Sauce (page 41). Redcurrants are very high in pectin. You may omit the spices if preferred.

> 1.5 kg (3 lb) redcurrants, stalked
> 3 cloves
> 6 cardamom seeds
> 3 cups (26 fl oz) water
> 1 cup (9 fl oz) white wine vinegar
> 6 cups (2³/₄ lb) sugar

Put the currants and spices into a saucepan with the water, and simmer until the currants are soft. Strain the mixture through a jelly bag. It will take 1 to 2 hours. Add the vinegar to the mixture and bring to the boil. Add the sugar, stirring until it dissolves, then boil rapidly until the setting point is reached. Bottle in sterilised jars immediately, label and seal.

Quince Jelly

A classic, old-fashioned jelly that will delight your friends. It has a beautiful colour and a rich subtle flavour. Serve with meats as well as bread and toast.

> 1 kg (2 lb) quinces
> $^1/_2$ cinnamon stick
> 6 cups ($2^3/_4$ imp. pts) water
> Sugar to measure

*R*ub the furry down off the quinces and cut them up into smallish pieces. Put them into a saucepan with the cinnamon and water. Bring to the boil and simmer until the fruit is tender. Strain the juice through a jelly bag into a bowl. It will take 1 to 2 hours. Measure the amount of cups the juice makes, you will need the same amount of sugar. Put the juice back into the saucepan and slowly bring to the boil. Stir in the sugar and keep stirring until it is dissolved. Bring the jelly to a rolling boil and cook until the setting point is reached. Pour the jelly into sterilised jars, label and seal.

Orange Jelly Marmalade

This is a more complicated recipe to make but visually it is the most beautiful.

> 4 oranges
> 2 lemons
> 9 cups (4 imp. pts) water
> Sugar to measure

A dish of Marinated Black Olives (page 77) on the outdoor table—the start of an alfresco lunch. Crusty country bread, spinach and pork pâté, a tomato salad, fig conserve and a bottle of wine will complete a quickly prepared lunch from the pantry.

*R*emove the peels of the fruit with a vegetable peeler. Shred the peel finely. Cut up the rest of the fruit and pith coarsely. Put all of the fruit apart from the shredded peel into a pan with 6 cups of water. Cover and cook for 2 hours. In the meantime, cook the shredded peel in 3 cups of water for $1^1/_2$ hours. Drain the liquid from the shreds and add it to the pulp in the pan. Strain the bulk of the fruit and juice through a jelly bag and allow to drip into a bowl for an hour. Measure the juice into a pan and for every cup of juice set aside one cup of sugar. Bring the juice slowly to the boil, add the sugar and stir until it is dissolved, then add the shreds and boil rapidly until setting point is reached. Remove from the heat and let the marmalade stand until a skin begins to form. Stir gently and ladle into warm, sterilised jars. Do not move the bottles until you are sure the jelly has set firmly. Seal, label and store in a cool, dark place.

Grape Jelly

Try this with black grapes as well and add half a cup of brandy to the jelly after setting point is reached. Delicious. Use this jelly to spread on Fruit Tarts (page 155), especially a grape tart.

> 1.5 kg (3 lb) green grapes
> $1^1/_4$ cups (11 fl oz) dry white wine
> 3 apples, sliced
> 1 lemon, thinly sliced
> 1 cinnamon stick
> 3 cloves
> Sugar to measure

*P*ut the grapes, wine, apples, lemon and spices in a pan, bring to the boil and simmer for about half an hour or until the fruit is tender. Strain the juice through a jelly bag into a bowl. It will take 2 hours. Measure the amount of cups the juice makes as you will need the same amount of sugar. Put the juice back into the saucepan and slowly bring to the boil. Stir in the sugar and keep stirring until it is dissolved. Bring the jelly to a rolling boil. Boil until setting point is reached. Pour the jelly into sterilised jars, label and seal.

Cherry Conserve

It is important to cook the conserve long enough so that it becomes a thick, luscious sauce. Easier to make than the jams and jellies. Bottle the same way.

2 oranges, thinly sliced with peel on
3 tablespoons water
750 g (1¹/₂ lb) cherries, stemmed
   and stoned
Juice of 3 lemons
3 cups (1¹/₂ lb) sugar
8 cardamom seeds
4 cloves

*P*ut the oranges and water into a pan and bring to the boil. Cook until the fruit is tender. Add the rest of the ingredients. Mix well, bring to the boil, and boil rapidly until the conserve is thick and clear. Pour into warm, sterilised pots and seal.

Fig Conserve

1 kg (2 lb) green or purple figs,
   quartered
Juice and peel of 3 lemons
1 cinnamon stick
3 cloves
4 cups (2 lb) sugar, warmed

*P*ut the figs in the pan with the lemon and spices and cook slowly until the figs are tender. Add the warmed sugar to the pan and slowly bring to the boil. Boil rapidly until setting point is reached. Pour into warm, sterilised pots and seal.

Lemon Curd

The egg yolks make the lemon curd a rich spread for toasts and cake but also limit its shelf life. It should be eaten within 2 months. Keep refrigerated. Use it also to spread on pre-baked lemon meringue pie tart shells, or make the Lemon Curd Pudding recipe following. Make lime curd or orange curd exactly the same way.

6 egg yolks
1 cup (7 oz) caster sugar
Zest and juice of 4 lemons
¹/₂ cup (4 oz) butter, cubed

*P*lace the yolks and sugar in the top of a double boiler or a bowl on top of simmering water. Stir frequently until the mixture thickens. Beat in the lemon, then gradually add the butter. Stir constantly for about 20 minutes until the mixture is very thick. Pour the curd into sterilised jars and seal when cool. Makes about 3 cups.

Lemon Curd Pudding

An easy recipe to make with pantry ingredients.

> 6 thin slices of stale bread, crusts
>   removed
> ¹/₂ cup (5 oz) Lemon Curd (see
>   preceding recipe)
> 2 eggs
> ¹/₃ cup (3 oz) caster sugar
> Peel of 1 lemon, grated
> 1¹/₄ cups (11 fl oz) milk, warmed

Spread the bread slices with lemon curd. Double grease a pudding basin with butter. Line the basin with the bread. Beat the eggs with the sugar and peel and gradually add the warm milk. Stir until the sugar has dissolved and the custard is thick, then pour over the bread in the bowl. Cover the top of the basin with 2 layers of aluminium foil and secure with string. Steam for 1 hour before serving. Serves 6.

Fruit in Alcohol

Poached fruits in sugar syrup and a spirit such as brandy or Armagnac are one of the greatest desserts. They seem to have lost favour so here is a chance to remind yourself of the perfection of poached fruits. No need to remind you how handy they are sitting in rows in your pantry just waiting for you to reach for them. The resulting syrup is actually a fruit liqueur so you are really making two delicious things to eat and drink.

Cherries in Kirsch

Serve in their liqueur with cream or ice-cream. The cherries may also be used for filling tarts; use the leftover liqueur for fruit punches. Do not open for 2 months.

> 2 kg (4 lb) cherries
> 2 cups (1 lb) sugar
> ¹/₂ cup (4 fl oz) water
> 1 cinnamon stick
> 3 star anise
> 1 teaspoon pepper
> 4 cups (1³/₄ imp. pts) kirsch

Cut the stems in half and put the cherries into the sterilised jars. Put the sugar, water and spices into a pan and bring to the boil. Remove from heat, let cool for 5 minutes and stir in the kirsch. Pour it over to cover the cherries and seal. About 8 serves.

Peaches in Brandy

> 2 kg (4 lb) peaches
> 2 cups (1 lb) sugar
> 2 cups (18 fl oz) water
> 1 cinnamon stick
> 3 cloves
> 6 cups (2³/₄ imp. pts) brandy

Scald the peaches in boiling water and skin them. Keep them whole if you want to keep the shape (they can get a bit ragged, halved, but then you can fit more in a jar). Prick each peach 8 times right through to the stone to enable the syrup to penetrate. Put the sugar, water and spices in a pan and bring to the boil. Let the peaches simmer in the syrup for 5 minutes only. Pack into sterilised jars with the spices. Reduce the syrup in half. Pour in the sugar syrup a third of the way up the bottles and top up with the brandy. Seal and keep for several months before opening. About 6 serves.

Quinces in Syrup

An unusual and lovely dessert.

1 kg (2 lb) quinces, peeled and cored
1 cup (8 oz) sugar
1¼ cups (11 fl oz) water
Juice and zest of 1 lemon
6 cardamom pods
3 cups (26 fl oz) flavourless vodka
    or gin

Cut the quinces into thick slices. Put the sugar, water, lemon and cardamom into a pan and bring to the boil. Add the quinces and let them simmer until the fruit is tender but not too soft. It may take up to an hour. Pack them into sterilised jars with the spices. Reduce the syrup if necessary—you only need enough to cover a third of each jar. Top up with vodka or gin. Keep for 2 months before opening. About 10 serves.

Preserved Lychees

It is good to see fresh lychees in the fruit markets in summer. Canned lychees bear no comparison with this delectable dessert.

1 cup (8 oz) sugar
2 cups (18 fl oz) water
1 tablespoon Szechuan peppercorns
1 kg (2 lb) fresh lychees, peeled
    and pitted
4 limes, thinly sliced
3 cups (26 fl oz) eau de vie or
    flavourless vodka

Put the sugar, water and pepper into a pan and bring to the boil. Add the lychees and limes and bring back to the boil, then remove pan from the heat. Pack the fruit into sterilised jars. Reduce the syrup if necessary as it only has to come a third of the way up the jars. Top up with eau de vie, seal and store. About 10 serves.

Tamarillos in Raspberry Liqueur

10 firm tamarillos, washed and
    stemmed
1 cup (8 oz) sugar
1 cup (9 fl oz) water
6 cloves
2 cups (18 fl oz) raspberry liqueur
1 cup (9 fl oz) eau de vie or vodka

Halve the tamarillos by cutting horizontally through the centre. Put the sugar and water into a pan and bring to the boil. Simmer and add the tamarillos and cloves. Cook for 5 minutes and remove from heat. Pack the tamarillos and cloves into sterilised jars. Add the raspberry liqueur and the eau de vie to the syrup and pour over the fruit. Seal and store for 2 months. 5 serves.

Pineapple in Rum

Use white or brown rum for this nostalgic dessert.

2 pineapples, top only removed
2 cinnamon sticks
3 cups (1½ lb) sugar
3 to 4 cups (26 to 35 fl oz) rum

Put the pineapples, cinnamon and sugar in a pan with enough water to just cover the pineapples. Simmer until the pineapple is tender. Drain and reserve the syrup. Peel and slice the pineapple and remove the core. Pack the rings into sterilised jars just a bit wider than the slices. Reduce the syrup down to 1 cup. Mix with the rum and pour over the pineapple. Seal and store for a month. About 12 serves.

Pineapple in Rum (this page), a delicious stand-by dessert that is very popular at our place. If you do not drink the leftover rum, store more pineapple slices in it, and omit adding the sugar syrup.

Grapes in Armagnac

This dessert is a great favourite in our family. It is so easy to make and is a great stand-by. Serve alone or with vanilla ice-cream or cream. The liqueur makes a nice little apéritif with a couple of grapes floating on the top.

1 kg (2 lb) large, firm grapes
1¹/₂ cups (11 oz) caster sugar
4 tablespoons water
1 tablespoon coriander seeds
Peel of ¹/₂ orange
1 bottle of armagnac

*W*ash and dry the grapes and cut them off the branches, leaving the stem on. Put the sugar and water into a pan and bring to the boil. Boil for 10 minutes. Pack the grapes, coriander and orange into sterilised jars. Mix the syrup and armagnac together and pour over the grapes. Seal and store for a few weeks. About 6 serves.

Prunes in Rum

You may be able to make this with your own dried plums (page 86).

2 cups (18 fl oz) water
4 Earl Grey tea bags
1 kg (2 lb) large, plump prunes
Peel of 1 lemon
¹/₂ cup (4 oz) sugar
2 to 3 cups (18 to 26 fl oz) white rum

*B*ring the water to the boil and pour over the tea bags in a bowl. Put in the prunes and leave to macerate for 12 hours. Pack the prunes into sterilised jars with a piece of the peel in each jar. Into a pan put the syrup and sugar and bring to the boil. Reduce if necessary. Allow to cool for 5 minutes. Pour the syrup a third of the way up the jars and top up with rum. Seal and store. They'll be ready to eat in a week. Serves 10.

Preserved Apricots

The syrup makes a delicious drink with soda water and some mint leaves.

2 kg (4 lb) apricots
1 kg (2 lb) sugar
5 cups (2 imp. pts) water
3 cloves
2 cups (18 fl oz) vodka

*P*rick the apricots about six times with a skewer right through to the stone. Put the sugar and water into a saucepan and bring to the boil. Add the apricots and cloves and as soon as it comes to the boil again take them out. Leave the apricots whole or cut them in half.

Bring the syrup to the boil again and continue to cook the syrup until it is nice and thick. Let it cool a little, add the vodka and pour over the apricots to cover them. Seal, label and store in a cool, dark place.

Mixed Berries in Rum

Served with ice-cream, yoghurt or just by itself, this is a heavenly dessert.

1¹/₂ cups raspberries, hulled
1¹/₂ cups strawberries, hulled
1 cup blueberries
1 cup (8 oz) vanilla sugar
3 cups (26 fl oz) white rum

*P*ut the fruits into a bowl. Sprinkle with the sugar and mix well. Put them into a sterilised jar and pour the rum over to cover the fruit. Seal and store for at least 4 weeks before eating.

Fruit Liqueurs

*T*hese are some of the simplest preserves to make. Liqueur is an infusion of fruit with 2 parts spirits to 1 part sugar. Sometimes you can also eat the fruit as an added bonus. Liqueurs are made with the cheapest spirits and fresh fruit and the miraculous change that takes place is always a delight. It is very useful to have a range of liqueurs in the pantry—the most useful being apricot, cherry, anise and blackcurrant (cassis). Natural fruit spirits like brandy are also useful but I'm not suggesting you can make those. Most handy in cooking are kirsch, brandy, calvados, framboise and slivovitz.

The syrup is made with a cup of sugar for a cup of water and cooked until the sugar dissolves. Spices and citrus peel can be added to vary the flavour. As a general rule the fruit is macerated in the sugar syrup and spirit for 1 or 2 months then strained and bottled.

Pawpaw Rum Liqueur

A tropical drink to sip at sunset on the verandah. Use like a cordial with soda water and plenty of ice.

4 cups (2 lb) pawpaw (papaya), peeled, seeded and cubed
1 cup (8 oz) sugar
1 cup (9 fl oz) water
Juice and peel of 1 lemon
4 cups (1³/₄ imp. pts) white or dark rum

*P*ut the pawpaw into a large jar. Make a syrup with the sugar, water and lemon by bringing to the boil and boiling for 10 minutes. Remove from heat, let cool, then pour over the pawpaw along with the rum. Seal and let the fruit macerate for 2 months. Strain into a bottle. Ready to drink. Makes about 7 cups.

Blueberry Brandy

Do not throw out the blueberries after straining to extract the liqueur. Serve them with ice-cream or use to fill Blueberry and Apple Pie (page 158). Delicious.

7 cups (1¹/₂ lb) blueberries
1¹/₂ cups (12 oz) sugar
Strip of orange peel
2 cinnamon sticks
4 cups (1³/₄ imp. pts) brandy

*P*ut the blueberries into a bowl and mash roughly with a potato masher. Mix in the sugar and place in a large, sterilised jar. Put the orange and cinnamon into the jar along with the brandy. Seal and store. Shake a few times in the first month, then let it rest for another month. Strain the liqueur into sterilised bottles and seal. Makes 4¹/₂ cups.

Summer Rum Pot

You need a large china pot, preferably with a lid, for this dish, which is a real moveable feast. The idea is you add to the pot as you have the fruits and, when it is full, cover and leave to macerate for three months before opening. Choose from strawberries, cherries (stoned), currants, raspberries, grapes, prunes, cumquats, and blackberries which should be whole. Cut peaches, apricots and plums in half, and quarter apples and pears.

2 cups (18 fl oz) white rum
3 cups (1¹/₂ lb) sugar
2 cups fruit

*P*ut the rum into the container with 2 cups of the sugar. Add the washed and dried fruit, stir and sprinkle on the other cup of sugar. Cover well. As other fruits become available, put them in and add sugar and rum in the same proportions as above.

Apricot Liqueur

This is excellent sprinkled over chilled sliced oranges or grapefruit; flame pancakes with it; add it to fruit salads, dry or fresh; pour it over ice-cream or sorbet. Oh yes—and drink it too!

> 500 g (1 lb) apricots
> 1 cup (8 oz) sugar
> 1 cup (9 fl oz) water
> $^1/_2$ vanilla pod
> 4 cups (1$^3/_4$ imp. pts) vodka

Halve the apricots and keep the stones. Prick each half 5 times right through with a skewer. Put the sugar and water in a pan and bring to the boil. Pack the apricots, stones and vanilla into a large jar. Pour the syrup over along with the vodka. Seal and store for 2 months. Strain the fruit and stones from the liqueur and bottle. You can put the $^1/_2$ vanilla bean into the bottle if you like. Makes 8 cups.

Peach Brandy

A delicious liqueur to make with a tray of peaches from the market. Save the perfect peaches for Peaches in Brandy (page 97) and use the rest for this. That should make some winter evenings warmer and brighter!

> 1 kg (2 lb) peaches, skinned and
>   stoned
> 1$^1/_2$ cups (12 oz) sugar
> 1 tablespoon chopped ginger
> 1 cinnamon stick
> 1 teaspoon peppercorns
> 4 cups (1$^3/_4$ imp. pts) brandy

Fruit Liqueurs are fascinating to experiment with— try out different fruits with vodka, gin or brandy and vary the spice mixture. Shown here is pale yellow Quince Liqueur (page 105) on the left; next to it is Apricot Liqueur (this page), with pear liqueur macerating in the background. Make quince and pear liqueur the same way as apricot liqueur. Wash the fruit, cut in halves or quarters. No need to remove seeds.

Slice the peaches and put into a bowl. Add the sugar and ginger and mix well. Put into a large sterilised jar, add the cinnamon, peppercorns and brandy. Seal and store for two months, shaking a few times in the first month. Strain the liqueur in a fine sieve and pour into sterilised bottles. Seal and leave for one month before drinking. Makes 4$^1/_2$ cups.

Blackberry Liqueur

Do not throw the blackberries away after straining. Eat them with ice-cream or purée and freeze to make a Granita (page 159).

> 7 cups (1$^1/_2$ lb) blackberries
> 2 cups (1$^1/_2$ lb) honey
> 1 tablespoon grated nutmeg
> 2 tablespoons peppercorns
> 4 cups (1$^3/_4$ imp. pts) brandy

Put the blackberries into a bowl and gently mash the fruit. Mix the honey and spices in. Put the fruit into a sterilised jar and pour the brandy over it. Seal and store for two months, shaking a few times in the first month. Strain the liqueur off through a fine sieve and bottle it. Seal and store. It will be ready to drink in a month. Makes 5 cups.

Cherry Liqueur

This is the most beautiful colour when held to the light in a fine liqueur glass. Use the dark red Morello cherries if you can get them.

> 2 kg (4 lb) cherries, stalks removed
> 1 cup (8 oz) sugar
> 1 vanilla pod
> 1 cinnamon stick
> 3 cups (26 fl oz) kirsch

Prick the cherries through to the stones with a fine skewer, six times each cherry. This helps the kirsch and sugar to penetrate the fruit. Put them in a bowl and mix the sugar into them. Transfer the cherries to a large, sterilised jar and put in the vanilla pod, cinnamon and the kirsch. Seal and store for 2 months, shaking a few times in the first month. Strain through a fine sieve into sterilised bottles. Makes 3 cups.

Four-Fruit Liqueur

Use the discarded fruit to make Granita (page 159)

> 1 kg (2 lb) cherries, stoned and
>   stalks removed
> 1 kg (2 lb) redcurrants, stalks
>   removed
> 1 kg (2 lb) strawberries, hulled
> 1¹/₂ cups (12 oz) sugar
> 1 tablespoon peppercorns
> 4 cups (1³/₄ imp. pts) eau de vie or
>   flavourless vodka

Put the fruit into a bowl and crush with a potato masher. Sprinkle in the sugar and pepper. Put the fruit into a large sterilised jar and pour the eau de vie over it. Seal and store for two months. Strain the liqueur into sterilised bottles. Ready to drink in a month but it will keep maturing, so try to be patient. Makes about 4 cups.

Orange Liqueur

A useful liqueur to use in sauces for all poultry and game, pork, ham and tongue. Goes very well with chocolate desserts and sweets, and with fruit dishes.

> 6 oranges
> 2 cups (1 lb) sugar
> 1 cinnamon stick
> 1 teaspoon coriander seeds
> 4 cups (1³/₄ imp. pts) white rum

Pare the zest from the oranges and put into a large jar. Remove the pith from the oranges, cut up the pulp and put it into the jar, discarding the pips. Put the sugar, spices and rum into the jar and leave to infuse for 2 months. Strain, squeeze and bottle. It is now ready to drink. Makes 7 to 8 cups.

Liqueur de Cassis (Blackcurrant Liqueur)

One of the most useful liqueurs in cooking as well as a pleasure to drink either neat or a spoonful with white wine or soda water.

> 4 cups (1¹/₂ lb) blackcurrants,
>   stemmed
> 1 clove
> A few blackcurrant leaves, if
>   possible
> 4 cups (1³/₄ imp. pts) brandy
> 2 cups (1 lb) sugar

Crush the blackcurrants with a fork and put with the other ingredients into a large jar and mix well. Seal and put away to macerate for 2 months. Strain through a jelly bag but *do* squeeze this time to get all the liqueur out. Siphon into a bottle. Ready to drink. Makes 7 to 8 cups.

Raspberry Liqueur

Try pouring this over a summer pudding or adding to a berry sorbet. Make strawberry liqueur exactly the same way.

> 500 g (1 lb) raspberries
> 1¹/₂ cups (12 oz) sugar
> ¹/₂ cup (4 fl oz) water
> 4 cups (1³/₄ imp. pts) eau de vie or
>   flavourless vodka

Crush the raspberries and put into a large jar. Put the sugar and water into a pan and bring to the boil. Boil for

5 minutes, allow to cool, then pour it over the raspberries along with the eau de vie. Allow to macerate in the pantry for 2 months. Strain into a bottle and seal. Ready to drink. Makes about 6 cups.

Mulberry Gin

A liqueur to make in early spring when mulberries start to appear. It is worth growing a mulberry tree just for this recipe alone.

> 7 cups (1¹/₂ lb) mulberries, stalks removed
> 1¹/₂ cups (12 oz) sugar
> 1 tablespoon coriander seeds
> 4 cups (1³/₄ imp. pts) gin

*M*ash the mulberries in a bowl. Dissolve the sugar over heat in a cup of water. Put the mulberries, sugar syrup, coriander and gin into a large sterilised jar to macerate for 2 months. Strain through a fine sieve into sterilised jars and seal. Try to keep for a month before opening. Makes about 5 cups.

Quince Liqueur

A heavenly drink to make from this exquisite fruit.

> 6 quinces, cut into 8
> 1¹/₂ cups (12 oz) sugar
> A few drops of almond essence
> 4 cups (1³/₄ imp. pts) flavourless vodka

*P*ut the quince into a sterilised jar. Make a syrup with the sugar and a cup of water and pour over the fruit along with the almond essence and vodka. Store for 2 months. Strain through a fine sieve into sterilised bottles and seal. Makes about 5¹/₂ cups.

Sage Liqueur

Herb liqueurs used to be served for medicinal purposes up until this century, and many's the time I've believed they were doing me good. Sage is believed to induce longevity, so don't say I didn't advise you.

> 1 packed cup sage leaves and flowers if available
> 2 cups (1 lb) sugar
> 4 cups (1³/₄ imp. pts) vodka

*P*ut the sage into a sterilised jar and make a syrup with a cup of water and the sugar. Pour the syrup over the sage along with the vodka. Seal and leave to macerate for 2 months. Strain into a sterilised bottle and seal. Makes 5 cups.

Anise Liqueur

Also known as anisette, aniseed or anis. A very popular seed for flavouring spirits in many different countries. Use it to flavour fruit desserts, or with fish and chicken dishes.

> 4 cups (1³/₄ imp. pts) flavourless tequila
> ¹/₂ cup (4 oz) anise seeds, crushed
> A small piece of cinnamon
> 2 tablespoons coriander seeds
> 2 cups (1 lb) sugar
> ¹/₂ cup (9 fl oz) water

*P*ut the tequila and spices into a large jar. Put the sugar and water in a pan and heat until sugar dissolves. Pour it over the tequila and mix well. Let it macerate for a month, strain and bottle. Ready to drink. Makes 6 cups.

4 *Pasta, Rice and Pulses*

*G*rains are the staple foods of most countries. There is couscous from the Middle East, rice and noodles from Asia, rolled oats from Scotland, pasta and polenta from Italy and endless varieties of breads from all over the world. They are an essential part of a pantry for everyday cooking and excellent for spontaneous alfresco meals. Dried beans and peas are really coming back into favour these days as we learn more about human nutrition. For centuries they were regarded as 'poor man's meat' because they are an excellent source of protein and were used by the poor as a substitute for meat. We are rediscovering that these simple regional foods are healthy and nutritious as well as tasty. Just combine with few spices, a few

Spicy Lentils (page 124) with lemon slices ready to serve, perhaps with some yoghurt and a fresh salad. They also make a delicious accompaniment to curry dishes.

106

vegetables, some sausage from confit or the freezer and you can have a splendid meal from your pantry at any time.

Noodles

*T*he Chinese have been eating noodles for over 3,500 years. The noodles come in varying degrees of thickness and are kept in long lengths as it is thought to symbolise and encourage long life. Noodles can be made out of wheat, rice and arrowroot or pea starch.

There are many varieties of noodles throughout the Asian world. They can be fried or served with a sauce of meat or vegetables.

To cook noodles. Allow one bundle of dried noodles per person. Put them in a bowl and pour boiling water over them. Allow to soak for 10 minutes, rinse and put into cold water until using them.

Chicken Noodle Soup

This soup is almost as fast to make as packet soup if you have a well-stocked pantry and some leftover chicken. Or make it with prawns for a change.

> 3 tablespoons Chinese dried mushrooms
> 4 bundles dried noodles, soaked
> 1 cooked chicken breast, shredded
> 3 cups (26 fl oz) Chicken Stock (page 28)
> 1 teaspoon Szechuan pepper
> 1 tablespoon light soy sauce
> 4 spring onions, finely chopped

*P*our a cup of boiling water over the mushrooms and soak for 30 minutes. Drain and reserve liquid. Put the drained noodles into a warm soup tureen. Cover with the chicken and mushrooms. Put the mushroom liquid and chicken stock in a pan and bring to the boil. Pour it in the tureen, season with pepper and soy, and garnish with spring onions. Serves 6.

Singapore Noodles

A delicious luncheon dish to make on the spur of the moment as most of the ingredients can be stored items.

> 4 tablespoons peanut oil
> 1 tablespoon Malaysian Curry Paste (page 54)
> 4 bundles dried noodles, soaked
> 2 eggs, beaten
> 250 g (8 oz) fresh or frozen peeled baby prawns
> 2 chillies, chopped
> 1 cup chopped spring onions
> 1 cup bean shoots
> 1 teaspoon sesame oil

*P*ut the peanut oil and curry paste into a wok and stir well for 1 minute. Add the noodles, eggs, prawns, chilli and $^2/_3$ of the spring onions and stir well. Cook for about 6 minutes until well combined. Add the bean shoots and cook for another few minutes. Sprinkle with sesame oil and the rest of the spring onions just before serving. Serves 4.

Pasta

Dried pasta is an ideal storage item. Pasta meals can be quickly assembled with delicious sauces made from items in your pantry—classic Italian sauces such as Baked Tomato Sauce (page 34), Pesto (page 38) or Anchovy Paste (page 36), which only take as long as the pasta to cook. Some-

times, just the addition of a fresh vegetable can make a world of difference to the flavour. Add lime and olives to the tomato sauce, grated zucchini to the pesto and broccoli to the anchovy paste. The sauces suggested here should go with most of the fascinating variety of pasta shapes.

To cook pasta. Put the dried pasta into a large volume of salted, boiling water for 15 to 20 minutes. Keep the water at a rolling boil throughout. Drain and mix with the sauce in a warmed bowl or put the pasta onto warm, individual plates and spoon the sauce on top. Serve freshly grated parmesan cheese separately—as a rule, 75 g (2$^{1}/_{2}$ oz) per serving.

Once you have mastered the technique of making fresh pasta you will find you can whiz some up without thinking about it. I don't recommend freezing it—the *raison d'être* of home-made is its freshness.

no longer sticks to your fingers. Cover with cling wrap and refrigerate for 1 hour.

Sprinkle flour on your work surface and roll out the pasta until very fine, about 1.6 mm ($^{1}/_{16}$ in.) thick. Now cut it into tagliatelle strips. I'd advise you to use a ruler. Cut wide strips for the first attempt, say 1 cm ($^{3}/_{8}$ in.) wide, gradually cut finer as you gain confidence. It still tastes as good. Put the strips onto racks to dry for an hour or two before cooking. Refrigerate after drying if not eating immediately.

Fresh Pasta

You can make this without fancy machines if you wish. Cook the same way as dried pasta but for only 5 to 6 minutes. It should still be a little firm, al dente.

> 2$^{1}/_{4}$ cups (9 oz) flour, sifted
> 3 egg yolks
> 1 tablespoon olive oil
> $^{1}/_{4}$ teaspoon salt
> 4 tablespoons iced water
> 30 g (1 oz) butter

*P*ut the flour on a cold work surface and make a well in the centre. Into it put the egg yolks, oil, salt and most of the water. Mix the centre items first, then gradually add the flour in from the sides. Keep mixing until you have a dough. Add more water if necessary. Work the dough with the palm of your hand until it is like an elastic ball and it

Pasta Sauces

These sauces serve 6 people. Use these recipes with fresh ingredients if preferred.

Tomato Sauce

> 1 tablespoon olive oil
> 2 cups Fresh Tomato Sauce
>   (page 32)
> $^{1}/_{4}$ cup (1 oz) slivered almonds,
>   chopped
> $^{1}/_{2}$ cup chopped basil

*H*eat the olive oil in a pan and add the other ingredients. Only cook a few minutes to heat it up and serve.

Tomato and Lime Sauce

Add the juice and zest of one lime to the recipe above.

Puttanesca Sauce

1¼ cups (11 fl oz) Baked Tomato
   Sauce (page 34)
⅓ cup (2 oz) capers
¾ cup (4 oz) black olives, pitted
1 chilli, chopped
2 tablespoons Anchovy Paste
   (page 36)
1 tablespoon olive oil
½ cup parsley, chopped

Put all the ingredients except parsley into a pan and simmer for 5 minutes. Garnish with parsley.

Zucchini and Pesto Sauce

1 tablespoon olive oil
500 g (1 lb) zucchini (courgettes),
   grated
¾ cup (7 fl oz) Pesto (page 38)
½ cup (2 oz) grated parmesan

Heat the oil and add the zucchini. Cook gently for 5 to 10 minutes until zucchini is soft. Quickly whirl in the pesto and allow to warm for a few minutes. Remove from heat and stir in the parmesan. Add a tablespoon of pasta water to thin out the sauce.

Broccoli and Anchovy Paste

2 cups (8 oz) small broccoli florets
2 tablespoons olive oil
3 tablespoons Anchovy Paste (page 36)
¼ cup (1 oz) grated parmesan cheese

Cook the broccoli for 7 minutes in boiling water and drain. Put the oil in a pan and add the broccoli and anchovy paste. Season and sauté for 5 minutes. Remove from heat, stir in the parmesan and serve.

Walnut Sauce

A quickly made pasta sauce with ingredients straight from the pantry.

3 slices stale bread, crusts removed
1 cup (9 fl oz) milk
345 g (11 oz) shelled walnuts
3 garlic cloves, crushed
½ cup (2 oz) grated parmesan
   cheese
5 tablespoons olive oil
1 teaspoon pepper

Soak the bread in the milk and squeeze. Put all the ingredients into the food processor and purée to a thick sauce ready to serve with pasta. Add some leftover milk if the sauce is too thick. Serves 4.

Asparagus and Artichoke Sauce

2 bunches of asparagus, snapped
4 tablespoons olive oil
345 g (11 oz) prosciutto, cut in
   bite-size pieces
12 artichoke quarters from
   Artichokes in Oil (page 74)
Juice and zest of 1 lemon
1 teaspoon each pepper and salt
2 tablespoons parsley, chopped

Cook the asparagus for 6 minutes in boiling water, refresh and cut into bite-size pieces. Heat the oil in a pan and add all the ingredients except for the parsley. Heat the vegetables through for about 6 minutes, stirring all the time. Remove from heat, spoon onto pasta and garnish with parsley. Serves 6.

The makings for Puttanesca Sauce (this page) in a saucepan, ready to be heated up in a few minutes and spooned over pasta. Out of the pantry came the Baked Tomato Sauce (page 34), capers, black olives, chilli and olive oil. You can add Anchovy Paste (page 36) as well to make it more authentic.

Chickpea and Chicken Sauce

A good pasta sauce to make with some leftover chicken, especially if you already have some chickpeas soaking.

- 3 tablespoons olive oil
- 1 onion, chopped
- 1¼ cups (8 oz) chickpeas, soaked
- 1 cup cooked chicken, shredded coarsely
- 3 garlic cloves, crushed
- 1 tablespoon thyme, chopped
- 2 chillies, chopped
- 1 teaspoon pepper
- 1 cup (9 fl oz) Chicken Stock (page 28)

Heat the oil in a pan and cook the onion until golden brown. Add all the other ingredients. Cook for about 15 minutes until the chicken stock is reduced by half. Serves 4.

Mushroom and Olive Sauce

Olives and mushrooms taste delicious together. If you have Duxelles (page 35) already made, you can make the sauce with half a cup of that instead of fresh mushrooms; or use dried mushrooms instead.

- 250 g (8 oz) mushrooms, thinly sliced
- 2 tablespoons olive oil
- 2 garlic cloves, chopped
- ½ cup Olive Paste (page 77)
- ¼ teaspoon cayenne
- ½ cup (2 oz) grated parmesan
- 4 tablespoons chopped chervil

Sauté the mushrooms in the oil until they are tender, then add the garlic, olive paste and cayenne. Stir for 5 minutes. It's now ready to serve over pasta garnished with parmesan and chervil.

Baked Macaroni

A great family dish for Sunday night when you think the cupboard is bare.

- 500 g (1 lb) macaroni
- 3 tablespoons butter
- 1 cup (9 fl oz) Fresh Tomato Sauce (page 32)
- 1 teaspoon pepper
- 250 g (8 oz) mozzarella cheese, thinly sliced
- ½ cup (2 oz) grated parmesan cheese

Cook the macaroni for 15 minutes—it should be more underdone than usual. Drain and mix with 2 tablespoons of the butter. Put half the macaroni in the dish. Top with half the tomato and half the pepper and mozzarella. Repeat. Sprinkle the parmesan on top and dot with the rest of the butter. Bake in a preheated oven 190°C (375°F) for 40 minutes or until the top is lightly browned.

Polenta

Polenta is roughly ground cornmeal. Polenta bread is made by boiling until it is stiff like a porridge, then pouring onto a flat surface to set. It makes a deliciously simple dish to serve with meats and poultry or with a salad for a casual lunch. Try it also with Olive Paste (page 77) and Spicy Tomato Sauce (page 34).

- 500 g (1 lb) polenta
- 6 cups (2¾ imp. pts) water
- ¼ cup (2 oz) olives, pitted and halved
- Olive oil

Put the polenta and water into a large pan and slowly bring to the boil, stirring often. Simmer for 30 minutes, stirring all the time to prevent the polenta from sticking. When thick, add the olives and stir. Pour into a well-oiled gratin dish and turn out when cold. It can be grilled or fried if liked. Please yourself how thick you make it. Serves 8.

Semolina

Semolina Gnocchi

Italian dumplings are simple to make and can be eaten as a starter or for a light lunch. They can also be made from potato or polenta. Semolina is made from hard wheat.

1 litre (1³/₄ imp. pts) milk
1 bay leaf
1¹/₂ cups (8 oz) semolina or polenta
¹/₄ teaspoon salt
1 teaspoon pepper
¹/₂ teaspoon dry mustard
³/₄ cup (3 oz) grated parmesan
   cheese
60 g (2 oz) butter

*H*eat the milk with the bay leaf slowly and bring to the boil. Remove the bay leaf and add the semolina, salt and pepper. Keep simmering for 15 to 20 minutes, stirring from time to time. Remove from heat and stir in the mustard and half the cheese and butter. Spread to about 1 cm (³/₈ in.) thick with a palette knife. When cold, cut it into 5 cm (2 in.) circles or squares with a knife. Arrange them in a buttered gratin dish, slightly overlapping each other in a single layer. Sprinkle with the remaining cheese and butter. Put into a preheated oven 200°C (400°F) for 25 minutes or until the top is golden brown. Serves 4.

Variation: Spoon Baked Tomato Sauce (page 34) over the top, then sprinkle with parmesan, but not the butter. Follow the recipe above to finish. Try with Pesto (page 38) as well.

Couscous

Couscous is one of the great dishes of northern Africa. It is grains of semolina, made from hard wheat. It is served with spicy meat and vegetable dishes accompanied by Harissa (page 54) or Hot Couscous Sauce (page 55).

The instructions on the packets of couscous are usually for a fast method of cooking. Though the result is good, it isn't nearly as wonderful as the traditional, slow method of steaming couscous which produces soft, fluffy grains. In Morocco, they cook their couscous in a special steamer—the couscoussier. A savoury meat or vegetable dish cooks in the bottom of the pot and the couscous cooks in a perforated steamer that sits up under the lid. You can make your own steamer just as well by fitting a colander or sieve into the top of a large pot so you can put the lid on without any steam escaping. Wrap a tea-towel around any gap.

To cook couscous. Cover the couscous with cold water, drain and let stand for 15 minutes to swell. Put the couscous in the muslin-lined colander over 4 cups of boiling water or stock and cover. Steam for 15 minutes and turn the colander onto a plate. Fork it over to break up any lumps and sprinkle with a little water. Return the couscous to the colander and steam for 30 minutes. Put the couscous onto a plate and melt 125 g (4 oz) butter or Smen (page 22) into the grains. Toss with a fork and serve.

Freezer Tip: Thawing. When thawing, most bulky items need 12 hours in the refrigerator so they gradually defrost and can then be left outside for a few hours to come to room temperature. To thaw faster, use the microwave or place the well-wrapped item in a bowl of warm water.

Couscous with Lamb and Vegetables

This will cause a sensation at a dinner party. Heap the steamed couscous up in a ring on a hot serving plate. Transfer the meat into the centre of the mound and then surround the mound with the vegetables, arranging the colours and shapes attractively. Garnish with coriander. Serve with Harissa (page 54) or Hot Couscous Sauce (page 55).

> 2 kg (4 lb) lamb shoulder, trimmed
>   and cut into bite-size pieces
> 750 g (1¹/₂ lb) couscous
> 125 g (¹/₄ lb) smen or butter
> Stock
> 2 tablespoons olive oil
> 2 onions
> 2 garlic cloves
> 2 cinnamon sticks
> 1 teaspoon salt
> 1 teaspoon pepper
> 3 chillies
> ¹/₂ teaspoon saffron
> Vegetables
> 8 medium carrots
> 8 thin eggplants (aubergines)
> 8 small parsnips
> 8 zucchini (courgettes)
> 8 spring onions
> 8 tomatoes, halved
> Coriander leaves to garnish

Put the lamb in the bottom of a pot and add all the stock ingredients. Cover with 1 litre (2 pts) water, cover and slowly bring to the boil. Skim and simmer, covered, for 30 minutes. Begin to prepare the couscous (this page). The lamb will take 1¹/₂ hours to cook, so after 1 hour put the vegetables in the stock. Serves 8.

Tabbouleh Salad

A well-known salad from the Middle East made up of parsley, mint and cracked wheat. To serve, heap up the salad in the middle of a large, round plate. Surround with small lettuce leaves or vine leaves to scoop up the salad. Decorate with olives for an extra garnish if liked.

> 1 cup (6 oz) fine cracked wheat
>   (burghul)
> 3 tablespoons finely chopped spring
>   onions
> 1¹/₂ cups finely chopped parsley
> ¹/₂ cup finely chopped mint
> 1 tomato, finely chopped
> 3 tablespoons olive oil
> 1 tablespoon lemon juice
> Salt and pepper
> Lettuce or vine leaves

Soak the burghul in water for half an hour. Drain and dry. Combine the burghul, spring onions, parsley, mint, tomato, oil and lemon juice. Add salt and pepper to taste. Serve with the leaves. Serves 4.

Cracked Wheat Stuffing for Roast Chicken

Known also as kibbled wheat or burghul or bulgar, cracked wheat makes a delectable stuffing with dried apricots for a roast duck or chicken. Soak in warm water for 30 minutes to soften and swell the grains.

> 1 onion, chopped
> 2 tablespoons olive oil
> 2 cups (12 oz) cracked wheat,
>   soaked and drained
> 2 tablespoons pine nuts
> 10 dried apricots, cut in strips and
>   soaked
> 1 tablespoon cumin seeds
> 1 tablespoon ground cinnamon

2 teaspoons pepper
5 tablespoons chopped parsley
1 chicken
Oil for brushing

Cook the onion in the oil until golden brown. Combine all the stuffing ingredients in a bowl and mix well. Stuff the chicken with the mixture and secure the opening. Brush the chicken with oil. Place the chicken on a rack over a baking dish and bake in the oven at 200°C (400°F) for 1$^{1}/_{4}$ hours or until you can pierce the flesh in the thigh and the liquid is clear, not pink. Serves 5 to 6.

Rice

The great staple food of two-thirds of the world, rice can be savoury, sweet or spicy. There are thousands of variations according to cuisine, just as there are many varieties of rice itself.

To cook rice: Rice is best cooked by the absorption method. Put one part rice to two parts of cold, salted water into a pan and bring to the boil. Stir, cover and turn the heat down as low as possible. You need a tight-fitting lid for cooking rice so no steam escapes. It will be ready in 20 minutes and the rice will have absorbed all the water. (Brown rice and wild rice will take 10 to 15 minutes longer.) Fork up the rice ready to serve. When cooking Basmati rice from India or Pakistan, wash the rice thoroughly under running water before cooking.

Short-grain rice is a good all purpose rice. Use long-grain rice and Basmati rice for pilaus, pilafs, salads and stuffings. Arborio is the Italian risotto rice. Use it also for paella, jambalaya and desserts. Wild rice is expensive but definitely worth eating occasionally. I like to stuff poultry and game birds with it.

Brown rice is much more nutritious than the hulled, white rices. It has nutty flavour which I find most pleasing.

Rice and Herb Salad

A refreshing herbed salad for summer lunches in the garden.

1 onion, chopped
2 tablespoons olive oil
*2 teaspoons Garam Masala
 (page 46)*
1 teaspoon turmeric
1 teaspoon pepper
1 tablespoon desiccated coconut
1 cup (5 oz) long-grain brown rice
*2 cups (18 fl oz) Chicken Stock
 (page 28)*
Juice and zest of 1 lemon
2 tablespoons olive oil
2 tablespoons chopped dill
2 tablespoons chopped coriander
2 tablespoons chopped parsley
2 tablespoons chopped hazelnuts

Sauté the onion in the oil until it is golden brown and add the garam masala, turmeric, pepper, coconut and rice. Cook, stirring for several minutes. Put in the chicken stock, stir and bring to the boil. Stir once, lower heat to simmer and cover. Cook for 25 minutes. Remove from the heat, fork through and lay out on a large plate so the rice doesn't stick together too much. When cool, add the lemon, oil, herbs and hazelnuts. Serves 4.

Rice and Bean Soup

3 bacon rashers, diced
1 onion, chopped
2 celery stalks, chopped
2 tomatoes, peeled and chopped
1 cup (6 oz) cannellini beans,
    soaked
Bouquet Garni (page 88)
7 cups (3 imp. pts) Chicken Stock
    (page 28)
1 teaspoon pepper
1 cup (5 oz) rice
$^1/_2$ cup (2 oz) grated parmesan

Heat the bacon until the fat runs out and add the onion. Cook until translucent and add the celery and tomatoes. Stir. Cook for 2 more minutes then add beans, bouquet garni, chicken stock and pepper. Stir and, when boiling, reduce to a simmer and cover. Cook for $1^1/_2$ hours or until beans begin to soften. Add the rice and more water if necessary. It will be ready in 15 minutes. Serve with parmesan cheese. Serves 6.

Dolmades (Rice-Stuffed Vine Leaves)

These delicious little parcels of savoury rice in vine leaves excel as a snack or appetiser.

Large vine leaves, fresh or tinned
2 tablespoons olive oil
2 onions, finely chopped
$1^1/_4$ cups (8 oz) rice
$^1/_2$ cup (2 oz) pine nuts
$^1/_2$ cup (2 oz) sultanas
2 tablespoons chopped green olives
1 teaspoon pepper
2 tablespoons olive oil
Juice of 1 lemon

If the leaves are fresh, blanch them in boiling water for a few minutes and refresh.

Put the oil in the pan and simmer the onions until golden. Add the rice, pine nuts, sultanas, olives and pepper and cook for a few minutes, stirring continuously. Add 2 cups of water, bring to the boil and then lower heat to simmer, and cover. In 15 to 20 minutes, the rice will be cooked. Fork it through, add some of the oil and lemon juice and stir until absorbed.

To stuff the vine leaves, put a teaspoon of rice mixture at the large end of the leaf (which you've placed shiny-side down). Roll up like a little parcel, tucking in the ends near the beginning. Pack them tightly into a shallow cake pan so they can't dislodge. Pour over the rest of the oil and lemon juice and a cup of water. Cover. Steam them or put in a preheated oven at 150°C (300°F) for an hour.

Sweet Turkish Pilaf

A beautiful, sweet rice to serve with spicy lamb stews or roast chicken.

2 tablespoons butter
3 spring onions, chopped
$1^1/_2$ cups (8 oz) long-grain rice
4 carrots, grated
2 tablespoons sultanas
1 teaspoon pepper
1 teaspoon cumin seeds
$^1/_2$ teaspoon saffron threads, soaked
3 cups (26 fl oz) Chicken Stock
    (page 28)
$^1/_2$ cup (3 oz) chopped cashew nuts

Heat the butter and add the spring onions. Cook for a few minutes and add the rest of the ingredients except the nuts. Stir and bring to the boil. Lower the heat to simmer, cover and cook for 25 minutes. Fork through the rice and sprinkle the cashews over when serving. Serves 4.

Rice Mould with Meat and Nuts

Serve this as a party dish to accompany the main courses.

> 2 cups (10 oz) long-grain rice
> 1 teaspoon turmeric
> 250 g (8 oz) minced (ground) lamb
>   or beef
> 1/2 cup (3 oz) pine nuts
> 1/2 cup (3 oz) pistachio nuts
> 3 tablespoons olive oil
> 1 teaspoon salt and pepper
> 1 teaspoon cumin
> 1 teaspoon cinnamon
> 1/4 cup (1 1/2 oz) sultanas
> Coriander leaves to garnish

Cook the rice and turmeric by the absorption method (page 117). Fry the meat and nuts in the oil for 10 minutes. Season with spices and sultanas.

Pack the rice firmly, while warm, into a warmed, greased mould or basin. Turn it out by placing a plate over the mould and turning it over. The rice should come out firmly moulded. Put the meat and nut mixture in the centre of the mould or around the edges. Garnish with coriander. Serves 8.

Prawn (Shrimp) Jambalaya

This wonderful party dish from New Orleans is a relative of the Spanish paella. Crusty bread, salad and a glass of wine or two is all that is needed for this hearty dish. I find it easiest to make it in my wok.

> 2 onions, finely chopped
> 3 tablespoons olive oil
> 4 garlic cloves, finely chopped
> 1 leek, finely chopped
> 1 red and 1 green capsicum
>   (sweet pepper), cut into strips

> 1 1/2 cups (8 oz) long-grain rice
> 3 cups (26 fl oz) Chicken Stock
>   (page 28)
> 2 tomatoes, peeled and chopped
> 1 1/2 tablespoons thyme, chopped
> 3 chillies, chopped
> Salt and pepper
> 1/2 teaspoon saffron, soaked
> 500 g (1 lb) green prawns,
>   deveined
> 250 g (8 oz) shelled mussels
> Lemon wedges to garnish

Cook the onions in the oil until golden. Add the garlic, leek and capsicum and stir for a few minutes. Put in the rice and stir until coated in oil. Add the stock and bring to the boil, stirring once. Add the tomatoes, thyme, chillies, salt, pepper and saffron, bring to the boil, then lower the heat to simmer. Cover tightly and cook for 20 minutes. Add the prawns and mussels by forking through the rice and inserting the seafood. Cook for 5 to 10 minutes. Serve from the wok or piled onto a large serving dish. Surround with lemon wedges. Serves 6 to 8.

Apple Risotto

This makes a splendid luncheon dish, served with a salad. I often make it as a safe standby meal from the pantry.

> 6 cups (2 3/4 imp. pts) Chicken
>   Stock (page 28)
> 3 tablespoons butter
> 2 cups (12 oz) arborio rice
> 6 apples, peeled and sliced
> Lemon peel
> Salt and pepper
> 1/2 teaspoon grated nutmeg
> 1 1/2 cups (13 fl oz) white wine
> 1/2 cup (2 oz) grated parmesan
>   cheese

*H*eat the chicken stock and keep simmering. Melt the butter and stir in the rice. Stir for a minute then add a ladle of hot stock. Stir again. Keep stirring every few minutes and add a ladleful of stock each time the liquid begins to dry out. After 15 minutes, add the apples, lemon peel, salt, pepper and nutmeg. Stir. When the stock is finished, add the wine. The risotto should take 25 to 30 minutes to be cooked but slightly firm. It shouldn't be dry. If you run out of liquid, add water so it is slightly sloppy. Stir in the parmesan at the end and serve in heated, shallow soup plates. Serves 6 to 8.

M u s h r o o m   R i s o t t o

This is one of the most splendid of rice dishes. It is a good idea to always have some packets of porcini, dried wild mushrooms from Italy, in the pantry. They add their fragrant flavour to soups, stews and sauces as well as risotto. Use a heavy-based pan. You could also use the dried mushrooms you made yourself (page 88).

> 30 g (1 oz) porcini mushrooms
> 4 cups (1³/₄ imp. pts) Rich Beef
>   Stock (page 28)
> 2 tablespoons butter
> 1 tablespoon olive oil
> 1 onion, finely chopped
> 1¹/₂ cups (9 oz) arborio rice
> 5 juniper berries
> ¹/₄ teaspoon saffron threads
> ¹/₂ teaspoon pepper
> Freshly shaved parmesan cheese

*S*oak the mushrooms in 2 cups of hot water for 30 minutes. Strain through a fine sieve and reserve the liquid. Add it

A classic Italian store cupboard dish—out come the arborio rice, onion and parmesan. The peas and Rich Beef Stock (page 28) or Chicken Stock (page 28) come out of the freezer.

to the stock and bring it to simmering point. Melt the butter and oil and add the onion. Cook until translucent. Add the rice and stir for a few minutes. Add ¹/₂ cup of the simmering mushroom stock. Keep stirring every few minutes and add ¹/₂ cup of stock every time the rice begins to dry out. Continue in this way for 10 minutes. Add the mushrooms, juniper berries and saffron, stir well and continue until the stock is used up. The risotto will take about 25 minutes. It should be thick, not runny, and the rice should be slightly firm. If by chance you need more liquid, add some hot water. Serve in individual warm bowls, a sprinkle of pepper and shavings of the cheese on top. Serves 6.

R i s i   e   B i s i
(R i c e   a n d   P e a s)

This is a thick Italian soup, a little like a risotto but much more runny.

> 2 tablespoons butter
> 1 onion, chopped
> 2 cups (12 oz) peas
> 4 cups (1³/₄ imp. pts) Rich Beef
>   Stock (page 28)
> 1 teaspoon salt
> 1 teaspoon pepper
> 1 cup (6 oz) arborio rice
> 2 tablespoons chopped parsley
> ¹/₂ cup (2 oz) freshly grated
>   parmesan cheese

*M*elt the butter, add the onion and cook until it is translucent. Add the peas and stir for a few minutes. Pour in the stock, salt and pepper and bring to the boil. Add the rice, stir and cover and cook for 20 minutes or until rice is tender. Just before serving, stir in the parsley and parmesan. Serves 4.

Rice and Chicken Salad

This is a lovely summer dish. It can be varied by adding prawns or lobster, fine slices of rare roast beef or sliced, cold sausages. Make this with barley for a change, or half and half.

3 cups (12 oz) cooked short-grain rice
$1/_2$ cup (2 oz) diced gruyère cheese
$1/_2$ cup (3 oz) black olives, pitted
  and halved
1 red capsicum, diced
3 tablespoons capers
2 half breasts cooked chicken, diced
3 tablespoons Vinaigrette (page 19)
$1/_4$ cup parsley, finely chopped

Put all the ingredients into a salad bowl and toss gently. Serve at room temperature. A sprinkle of paprika to garnish looks attractive. Serves 6.

Indian Spicy Rice with Peas

Peas and rice are a wonderful combination. I always keep a packet of frozen peas in the freezer as they are so handy for making dishes like this and Risi e Bisi (page 119). You can substitute $1/_4$ teaspoon saffron threads for the turmeric for special occasions and use chicken stock instead of water.

1 tablespoon mustard oil
5 whole cloves
12 peppercorns
6 cardamom pods
1 cinnamon stick
1 tablespoon coriander
1 tablespoon cumin
1 teaspoon turmeric
1 bay leaf
$1^1/_2$ cups (8 oz) long-grain or
  Basmati rice, washed
4 cups ($1^3/_4$ imp. pts) water
1 cup (6 oz) peas

Heat the oil in a pan and add all the spices and bay leaf. Keep cooking until they begin to expand, then add the rice. Stir for a few minutes, then add the water. Bring to the boil, add the peas and stir. Cover the pan and simmer for 20 minutes. Serves 8.

Indian Rice Soup

2 tablespoons butter
2 onions, chopped
2 garlic cloves, chopped
1 tablespoon Madrasi Masala
  (page 47)
1 teaspoon turmeric
1 cup (5 oz) long-grain or Basmati
  rice
5 cups ($2^1/_4$ imp. pts) Chicken
  Stock (page 28)
$1/_2$ cup (4 fl oz) Coconut Milk
  (page 25)
Zest of 1 lime
1 lime, thinly sliced
Coriander or mint to garnish,
  optional

Melt the butter and add the onions. Simmer until they are soft and add the garlic, Madrasi masala and turmeric. Cook, stirring all the while, for 5 minutes. Add the rice and stir for a minute, then pour in the chicken stock, coconut milk and lime zest. Bring to the boil and turn down to a simmer and cover. Cook for twenty minutes. When serving, float the lime slices on top. Garnish with herbs. Serves 6.

Torta di Riso (Rice Cake)

Rice makes a wonderful dessert, as you may remember if you ever had well-made baked rice and custard pudding as a child.

> 4 cups (1³/₄ imp. pts) milk
> Zest of ¹/₂ orange
> 1 cup (7 oz) Vanilla Sugar (page 4)
> ¹/₃ cup (2 oz) arborio rice
> 4 eggs
> ¹/₂ cup (2 oz) slivered almonds
> ¹/₃ cup (2 oz) sultanas
> ¹/₃ cup (2 oz) mixed citrus peel
> 2 tablespoons brandy
> 1 tablespoon dry breadcrumbs

Put the milk, orange and sugar into a pan and bring to the boil. Add the rice, cover and cook on the lowest heat for 2¹/₂ hours until the mixture is a mush. Beat the eggs and gradually beat in the rice a spoonful at a time. Add the almonds, sultanas, citrus peel and brandy and mix well. Grease a cake pan and sprinkle with the breadcrumbs. Pour the cake mixture in and bake in a preheated oven 180°C (350°F) for an hour. When it has cooled a little, turn onto a serving plate. Serve at room temperature. Serves 8.

Moroccan Rice Pudding

> 2 tablespoons raisins
> 2 tablespoons orange-flower water
> 4 cups (1³/₄ imp. pts) milk
> ¹/₂ cup (3 oz) short-grain rice
> 2 tablespoons ground rice
> ³/₄ cup (6 oz) Vanilla Sugar (page 4)
> 1 cup (4 oz) ground almonds
> 1 tablespoon ground cinnamon

Put the raisins in the orange-flower water to soak. Bring 3 cups of milk slowly to the boil in a saucepan. Add the rice and simmer for 15 minutes. Combine the ground rice with a little cold water to form a paste. Mix in the remaining milk. Pour this into the saucepan with the rice. Stir until it comes to the boil, add the sugar and almonds and simmer, stirring, until the mixture thickens. Remove from heat. Strain the raisins and stir the orange-flower juice into the rice. When cool, pour rice into a shallow bowl and refrigerate. Just before serving sprinkle with the raisins and cinnamon.

Dried Beans and Peas

These pulses are the dried seeds of podded plants and have been a staple food for thousands of years. They are a valuable source of protein and an excellent substitute for meat. Do not store them for more than a year as they become too hard and difficult to cook. Be sure to buy them from a reliable source.

To soak dried beans and peas. They need to be soaked for up to 6 hours before using. If you don't have time, put them in a pan of cold water, bring to the boil and simmer for 5 minutes. Cover the pan, remove from heat and let the peas or beans cool before cooking them. Alternatively, keep some cooked beans or peas in the freezer in cup portions. Always salt at the end of cooking. Use any kind of dried bean for these recipes —cannellini, navy, flageolets, lima or red kidney beans.

Haricot Bean Salad

2 cups (12 oz) dried haricot beans,
  soaked
Bouquet Garni (page 88)
4 garlic cloves, chopped
3 onions, chopped
3 carrots, chopped
2 tablespoons olive oil
Juice of 1 lemon
1 tablespoon mint
1 tablespoon parsley
1 tablespoon thyme
1 teaspoon salt
1 teaspoon pepper
$^{1}/_{4}$ cup (2 oz) black olives, pitted
  and halved

Put the beans and bouquet garni into
a pan and cover with water. Bring to
the boil, skim and cook for an hour.
Add the garlic, onions and carrots,
bring back to the boil, then simmer for
another hour or until the beans are tender. Drain and pour over the oil, lemon,
herbs, salt and pepper. Garnish with the
olives. Serves 6.

White Bean Soup

This is a hearty French country dish transformed into a party dish with the addition
of the duck confit.

2$^{1}/_{2}$ cups (1 lb) dried haricot beans,
  soaked
3 onions, diced
2 carrots, diced
3 tomatoes, skinned and diced
Bouquet Garni (page 88)
1 small pumpkin, diced
4 potatoes, diced
1 teaspoon salt
1 teaspoon pepper
2 confit duck legs (page 137), cut
  in 4

Drain the beans and put in a pan.
Cover with 3 litres (5$^{1}/_{2}$ imp. pts) of
water, bring to the boil and skim. Add
the onions, carrots, and tomatoes and
bouquet garni. Simmer for 1$^{1}/_{2}$ hours.
Add the pumpkin and potatoes and
cook for another 15 minutes. Add the
duck pieces, salt and pepper and cook
until everything is tender. Serves 8.

Black-Eyed Beans with Sausages

Just as good with lentils, chickpeas or split
peas.

2$^{1}/_{2}$ cups (1 lb) black-eyed beans,
  soaked
3 garlic cloves
1 bay leaf
2 teaspoons Ras el Hanout
  (page 43)
2 bacon rashers, chopped
6 Merguez Sausages (page 141) or
  spicy pork sausages

Put the beans, garlic, bay leaf and ras
el hanout in the pan and cover with
water. Bring to the boil, skim and simmer until the beans are tender (about
1$^{1}/_{2}$ hours). Put the bacon in a pan and
cook for a few minutes, then add the
sausages. Cook until they are done. If
there is any water left in the beans, drain
it off. Add the bacon and sausages and
serve. Serves 6.

White Bean Soup (this page) is a provincial soup
from the Basque area of France. It is rich and strongly
flavoured, especially with the addition of some pieces
of Duck Confit (page 137).

Cannellini Beans with Tuna

Any of the white beans will taste just as good with this recipe.

> 2¹/₂ cups (1 lb) cannellini beans, soaked
> Bouquet Garni (page 88)
> 2 onions, thinly sliced
> 185 g (6 oz) canned tuna, drained and forked
> 4 tablespoons olive oil
> 1 tablespoon balsamic vinegar
> 1 teaspoon salt
> 1 teaspoon pepper
> 2 tablespoons parsley

Put the beans and bouquet garni in the saucepan, cover with water and bring to the boil. Skim and then simmer until they are tender. Drain the beans, remove the bouquet garni and add the onions, tuna, oil, vinegar, salt and pepper. Mix well. Garnish with parsley. Serves 6.

Ful Nabed

A purée of dried white broad beans, very popular in the Middle East. Use it as dip with crudités and pita bread. Wedges of pita bread taste delicious grilled until almost black. I discovered this through sheer carelessness when I almost burnt the last of the pita bread. They are crispy and crunchy like potato chips but healthier.

> 1¹/₄ cups (9 oz) dried broad beans, soaked
> 2 onions, chopped
> Juice of 1 lemon
> ¹/₂ teaspoon salt
> ¹/₂ cup (4 fl oz) Moroccan Salad Dressing (page 19)
> Paprika to garnish

Put the beans and onions into a pan and cover with water. Bring to the boil and simmer for about 1¹/₂ hours or until tender. Drain the beans and blend them in the food processor. Add the lemon juice, salt and dressing and blend to a creamy paste. Put into a shallow dish. Garnish with paprika.

Pea and Ham Soup

An old favourite, this is the recipe I devised when I began to cook with reduced animal fat. I sometimes make this with 3 cups of split peas and ¹/₂ cup of barley. Fabulous texture, so do not purée on any account. It is a meal in itself.

> 2 smoked pork hocks
> Bouquet Garni (page 88)
> 3¹/₂ cups (1¹/₂ lb) dried split peas, soaked
> 4 onions, chopped
> 4 carrots
> 2 parsnips, chopped
> 5 celery sticks, chopped
> 1 teaspoon pepper

Make the stock the day before. Put the pork hocks and bouquet garni in a pot, cover with plenty of water and bring to the boil. Cook for 2 hours or until the hock is tender. Allow to cool. Drain the stock and put into the refrigerator. When the fat is set solid on top, remove it. Take off the skin of the pork and extract the meat and chop into cubes. Soak the peas.

The next day, drain the peas and put into a pan with the pork stock and enough water to more than cover the peas. Bring to the boil and add the pork meat, onions, carrots, parsnips, celery and pepper. Simmer until the peas and vegetables are tender, about 2 to 3 hours. You can purée it in a blender if liked but I prefer the mushy texture. Serves 6.

Dried Pea Purée

An old-fashioned dish to serve with hearty meals like Pickled Pork or Beef (page 138), Sausages (page 136) or roast duck. You can make it as a meal in itself by adding some chopped sausages or ham.

500 g (1 lb) split peas, soaked
1 onion, chopped
1 carrot, sliced
1 parsnip, sliced
Bouquet Garni (page 88)
1 tablespoon pepper
1 teaspoon salt
1 tablespoon butter
2 tablespoons chopped parsley

Put the peas into fresh water and bring to the boil. Remove any scum that comes to the surface over the next 15 minutes. Add the onion, carrot, parsnip and bouquet garni, pepper and salt. Cover and simmer until all is tender. Drain, remove the bouquet garni and blend in the food processor. Reheat with the butter. Sprinkle with parsley to serve. Serves 4 to 6.

Lentils

Lentils have all the advantages of dried peas and beans and an additional one—they don't have to be soaked. And they only take about 30 to 45 minutes to cook. Substitute lentils for beans in some of the recipes.

Spicy Lentils

2¹/₂ cups (1 lb) lentils
1 cinnamon stick
1 bay leaf
4 garlic cloves, crushed
2 tablespoons chopped ginger
1 teaspoon turmeric
1 lemon, sliced
1 teaspoon salt

1 teaspoon pepper
¹/₄ teaspoon cayenne
1 tablespoon mustard oil
1 tablespoon cumin seeds
5 cardamom pods

Put the lentils, cinnamon, bay leaf, garlic, ginger and turmeric into a pan and cover with water. Bring to the boil, cover and simmer until the lentils are tender, 30 to 40 minutes. Put the lemon, salt, pepper and cayenne into the pan, stir and leave for 5 minutes. Drain off any surplus liquid. Put the oil in pan, add the cumin and cardamom and fry until the seeds darken. Pour this over the lentils, mix well and serve. Serves 8.

Megadarra

I just loved this simple dish the first time I tasted it. Megadarra has proved to be a favourite with my friends as well. Serve it with a dish of yoghurt garnished with mint.

1¹/₄ cups (8 oz) lentils
2 onions, finely chopped
3 tablespoons olive oil
1¹/₄ cups (8 oz) long-grain rice
3 onions, finely sliced
2 teaspoons Ras el Hanout
   (page 43)

Place the lentils in a pan, cover with water, bring to the boil and simmer until cooked (about 40 minutes). Cook the chopped onions in the oil until golden brown, remove from oil and save the oil. Put the rice into a pan with 2¹/₂ cups of cold water and cook by the absorption method (page 115). Put the sliced onions into the pan with oil and cook until the onions are dark brown, almost caramelised. In a bowl, mix together the lentils, chopped onions, rice and ras el hanout. Garnish with the onion slices and pour the remaining oil over. Serves 6.

125

Lentil Soup

A rustic dish of very thick soup, it can be served as a main meal with crusty bread and a salad.

> 2 onions, chopped
> 6 Hungarian Sausages (page 141)
> 2 tablespoons olive oil
> 3 garlic cloves, crushed
> 2$^1/_2$ cups (1 lb) lentils
> 2 cups (18 fl oz) Rich Beef Stock
>   (page 28)
> 500 g (1 lb) spinach, chopped
> 4 potatoes, cubed
> 1 teaspoon Hot Sherry Vinegar
>   (page 17)
> 1 teaspoon salt

Fry the onions and sausages in the oil. Add the garlic and lentils and pour in stock and water to cover. Bring to the boil and simmer for 20 minutes. Add the spinach and potatoes, vinegar and salt. Cook for another 20 minutes or until everything is tender. Serves 6.

Tahini Sauce

Tahina paste is a Middle Eastern paste made from sesame seeds, rich in calcium and protein and very handy to have in the cupboard. Just mix with some lemon juice, cumin and parsley for a sauce for grilled vegetables or meatballs. Mixed with ground chickpeas it makes the well-known Hummus bi Tahina; mixed with baked eggplant, Baba Ghanoush. These sauces will last up to a week in the refrigerator. Use Tahini Sauce as a dip with pita bread or a sauce for meats and fish.

> 3 garlic cloves, crushed
> $^1/_2$ cup (4 fl oz) lemon juice
> $^1/_2$ cup (4 fl oz) tahina paste
> 1 teaspoon ground cumin seeds
> $^1/_2$ teaspoon salt, optional
> $^1/_2$ cup finely chopped parsley

Combine all the ingredients, except parsley, in the food processor and blend to a smooth paste. Salt if liked. Place the sauce in a bowl and sprinkle with the parsley just before serving. It can also be served with a sprinkle of olive oil and paprika. Makes 1 cup.

Tahini Sauce with Yoghurt
Add $^1/_2$ cup (4 fl oz) natural yoghurt to the recipe above. Makes 1$^1/_2$ cups.

Hummus bi Tahina (Chickpea and Sesame Paste)

This is a wonderful paste from the Middle East. It can be eaten as a dip or as a sauce to liven up fish and kebabs. Serve with pita bread. Homemade is best.

> 150 g (5 oz) chickpeas, soaked
> 4 tablespoons Tahini (this page)
> Juice of 2 lemons
> 4 garlic cloves, crushed
> 1 teaspoon salt
> 2 tablespoons olive oil
> 2 teaspoons cumin seeds
> 1 teaspoon paprika
> Sprigs of parsley to garnish

Cook the chickpeas in fresh water for about 1$^1/_4$ hours or until tender. Drain. Put all the ingredients except paprika and parsley into the food processor. Blend to a creamy paste. Serve on a plate dusted with paprika and decorated with parsley. Serves 4 to 6.

Tahini Sauce with Yoghurt (this page) is a refreshing, tasty dip to eat with fresh vegetables and pita bread. Sprinkle with paprika when serving.

Chickpeas

*C*hickpeas are a favourite food in Europe, the Middle East and India.

To cook chickpeas. They need to be soaked and cooked the same as dried beans (page 121). They can be (cooked and) served as a salad with vinaigrette or tomato sauce, added to casseroles, soups and couscous. You can fry them in oil, and season and eat them like nuts. They make the delicious dip Hummus (page 126). In India they are cooked with onion, garlic and chillies then fried with aromatic spices.

Chickpea Purée

Serve this purée with grilled meats, rissoles and sausages. Use split peas exactly the same way to serve with duck, lamb, ham or sausages.

> $2^1/_4$ cups (1 lb) chickpeas, soaked
> 100 g (4 oz) ham
> 1 onion, chopped
> 1 leek, chopped
> Bouquet Garni (page 88)
> 3 potatoes, chopped
> 3 tablespoons butter
> 1 teaspoon salt
> 1 teaspoon pepper

*P*ut the chickpeas into a pan, cover with water and bring to the boil, skim. Add the ham, onion, leek and bouquet garni. Simmer for $1^1/_2$ hours and add the potatoes. Keep simmering until all is tender. Blend in the food processor and add in the butter. Season. Serves 6.

Couscous with Lamb and Chickpeas

I buy a shoulder of lamb and mince the meat in the food processor. The lamb from the shoulder is so very tender that it is worth the effort of trimming off all the fat. Serve with Harissa (page 54) or Hot Couscous Sauce (page 55).

> 1 onion, chopped
> 1 teaspoon cumin seeds
> 1 bay leaf
> 750 g ($1^1/_2$ lb) couscous
> 250 g (8 oz) chickpeas, soaked
> 2 onions, finely chopped
> Olive oil
> 500 g (1 lb) minced lamb
> 4 garlic cloves, chopped
> 2 tablespoons tomato paste
> 3 tomatoes, peeled and chopped
> 2 teaspoons cinnamon
> 2 teaspoons cumin
> Salt and pepper
> 2 chillies, chopped
> 3 tablespoons Smen (page 22) or
>   olive oil

*P*ut 5 cups (2 imp. pints) of water in the bottom of the couscoussier or large pot. Add the 1 chopped onion, cumin and bay leaf and bring to the boil. Place the muslin-lined top of the couscoussier or sieve on top. Put in the couscous and chickpeas and cover tightly. Cook for one hour or until tender (see page 112).

In the meantime, cook the 2 chopped onions in the oil until translucent. Add the lamb and garlic and cook, stirring until the lamb is done. Stir in the to-mato paste, tomatoes and spices. Stir well for 5 minutes. Cover and keep in a warm place.

Put the couscous mixture onto a large, warm plate and add smen. Toss through the couscous and place the lamb mix-ture in the middle of the couscous mould. Serve immediately. Serves 6.

Harira
(Moroccan Soup)

A really popular dish to make straight from the pantry with the addition of a few fresh ingredients.

  1 cup (7 oz) chickpeas, soaked
  1 cup (7 oz) dried white beans,
    soaked
  500 g (1 lb) stewing lamb, cubed
  1 cup (7 oz) lentils
  3 tomatoes, peeled and chopped
  3 onions, chopped
  2 teaspoons Harissa (page 54)
  $^1/_4$ teaspoon saffron threads
  Juice of 1 lemon
  3 tablespoons flour
  1 cup coriander
  1 cup mint

Put the chickpeas, beans and lamb in a pan and cover with cold water. Bring to the boil and cook for $1^1/_2$ hours or until nearly tender. Add the lentils, tomatoes, onions, Harissa, saffron, and lemon juice and cook for 40 minutes until they are tender. Mix the flour with water to form a paste. Add some hot water from the chickpeas and mix well. Stir the paste into the chickpeas, simmer and stir until the liquid thickens. Add the herbs and cook for a further 10 minutes. Serves 10.

Chana Dhal with Eggplant

Chana dhal is a round yellow grain from the chickpea family and is hulled and split. Served hot or cold, it is a classic accompaniment to Indian curries. If you cannot get chana dhal, use small orange lentils

instead. *Make this dish with half rice and half chana dhal for a change and add a leek instead of the eggplant. Use Sambar Powder (page 47) as a variation from garam masala and omit the cayenne.*

  1 cup (6 oz) chana dhal
  2 tablespoons chopped ginger
  1 large eggplant (aubergine), cubed
  $^1/_2$ teaspoon pepper
  1 teaspoon Garam Masala
    (page 46)
  2 tablespoons lemon juice
  $^1/_4$ teaspoon cayenne
  1 tablespoon oil

Put the chana dhal, ginger and eggplant in a pan and cover with water. Bring to the boil and simmer for an hour. Drain. Add the remaining ingredients and mix well. Serves 4.

Barley Soup

A nourishing soup for wintry days.

  $^1/_2$ cup (3 oz) split peas, soaked
  2 onions, chopped
  Bouquet Garni (page 88)
  1 cup (6 oz) barley
  2 cups Beef Stock (page 28)
  8 cups ($3^1/_2$ imp. pts) water
  Salt and pepper
  3 carrots, chopped
  3 parsnips, chopped
  1 cup chopped parsley
  Extra 3 tablespoons chopped parsley

Put the split peas, onions, bouquet garni, barley, beef stock, water, salt and pepper into a large saucepan. Bring to the boil, cover and simmer for an hour. Add the carrots, parsnips and cup of parsley and simmer 45 to 60 minutes until all the vegetables are soft. Serve with the extra parsley sprinkled on top. Serves 6 to 8.

5 *Charcuterie, Fish, Cheese and Savoury Flans*

*P*ork and spinach pâté, pickled pork, cured ham, duck confit, pork rillettes, potted tongue, merguez and bratwurst sausages—all are charcuterie items. They are made from different meats but in particular, pork. It is a great art to prepare these meats well and fascinating to make at home. It can be difficult to find some of these foods and mostly they are very expensive, so even though you don't have to preserve meat from necessity, try them out for the delight of discovering new tastes.

Enjoy curing your own salmon or trout for your friends to enjoy, and you will never bother to buy cured salmon again. There are recipes for

Labna cheese (page 149) made from homemade yog-hurt which has been hung for 4 hours in layers of muslin to extract the whey, and then further compressed in a cheese mould. This is an antique mould of particular beauty. Watch out for them in antique shops.

making your own fresh cheeses and yoghurt and, for a meal in a flash, make an
onion flan from a homemade flan base
straight from the freezer or a pizza from
your frozen bread dough with bottled spicy
tomato sauce.

Pâtés and Terrines

The perfect picnic food laid out on a cloth
and surrounded by crusty bread, salad and
fruit. Pâté originally meant 'surrounded by
pastry', and today, by extension, it refers to
all kinds of charcuterie items made from
chopped or ground meat even though they
may not be covered in pastry. Terrine refers
to the earthenware mould the meat mixture
is cooked in, and is the term often used for
more coarsely ground pâtés.

The difference between a meat loaf and a
pâté is the cooking method. The meat loaf
is crusted on its sides when it bakes but the
pâté is baked in the terrine standing in a
dish of hot water which prevents it from
crusting. Sometimes the pâté is wrapped in
puff pastry and called pâté-en-croute.

Flavourings will vary the effect and
so will the texture of the meats—coarsely
cut or finely ground. You can use juniper
berries, cardamom, allspice, pepper, salt,
thyme, bay leaf, garlic, shallot, pistachio,
hazelnut, port, Madeira and, of course, Sel
Epicé (page 22).

It is worthwhile investing in one of the
very attractive terrine moulds available, as
it will look so wonderful on the table. Serve
with fresh crusty bread and Pickled Gherkins
(page 71)—some Pickled Onions (page 65)
would go well too. In fact, just glance along
your pickles and choose whichever one takes
your fancy.

Refrigerate for 3 to 5 days after it is made
to give the flavours time to amalgamate. It
will last about a week. Don't hesitate to
freeze a pâté as they are most successfully
frozen. If you do not want to freeze the
pâté, you can cook it in preserving jars in
a dish of hot water, the same way as in the
terrine dish. When the pâté is cooled, and
after the meat has been compressed, pour a
thick layer of lard over the top so that it is
completely sealed. When the lard has set
lay a cover of aluminium foil over the fat
and seal the lid. It will last a month in the
refrigerator. Alternatively, if you have the
French glazed earthenware pots use them,
as they were made for precisely this purpose.
Put an extra cover over the top and tie
with string, the way you cover jam. It
looks splendid on the table or to take to a
picnic.

Pâté de Campagne

This refers to a coarse, chunky-textured
pâté. There are hundreds of varieties.

250 g (8 oz) chicken livers
750 g (1½ lb) minced lean pork
185 g (6 oz) minced belly of pork
2 shallots, finely minced
1 teaspoon pepper
1 teaspoon salt
2 teaspoons Sel Epicé (page 22)
2 teaspoons chopped thyme
2 garlic cloves, chopped
2 tablespoons port
45 g (1½ oz) hazelnuts, roughly
    chopped
5 bacon rashers

Trim the chicken livers and mince
in the food processor. Combine all the
ingredients, except for the bacon, in a
bowl. Mix thoroughly so the meat
mixtures are embedded with the flavourings. I mix with my hands. Line
a terrine dish with the bacon, leaving
long ends hanging down at the sides

to fold over and seal the top. Press the meats in and arrange the bacon over the top. Put the lid on and place the terrine in a baking dish with 2.5 cm (1 in.) of hot water in it. Place in a preheated oven 180°C (350°F) and cook for 2 hours. Test with a skewer—if it comes out clean, the pâté is ready. Remove from heat, put some kitchen paper over the top and put some weights on top (e.g., tins of food) to compress the meats. Refrigerate when cool.

Duck Terrine

500 g (1 lb) duck meat
150 g (5 oz) chicken livers,
  trimmed
500 g (1 lb) pork mince
$^1/_2$ cup (4 fl oz) brandy
$^1/_2$ cup (4 fl oz) dry white wine
1 teaspoon salt
1 teaspoon pepper
1 teaspoon juniper berries
6 bay leaves

Mince the duck meat and chicken livers in the food processor. Mix all the ingredients together except for bay leaves. Press down into the terrine and smooth the top. Arrange the bay leaves over the top and cover. Put in a baking dish of hot water and put in a preheated oven 180°C (350°F) for 1$^1/_2$ hours. Test to see if it is done. Weight down until cool. Refrigerate.

Liver Pâté

Put this smooth and fine textured paste into small porcelain terrine moulds and keep in the refrigerator or freezer for when needed. They make a perfect starter with toast or water biscuits. A few marinated green olives or Olive Paste (page 77) would go nicely with it.

250 g (8 oz) calf's liver, deveined
250 g (8 oz) chicken livers,
  trimmed
$^1/_2$ cup (4 oz) butter
1 shallot, finely chopped
$^1/_2$ cup (4 fl oz) brandy
1 teaspoon salt
1 teaspoon pepper

Cut all the livers into small pieces. Melt a tablespoon of the butter in a pan and sauté the shallot until almost cooked. Put the livers in for a minute or two until they are cooked but still a little pink inside. Pour in half the brandy and the salt and pepper, let it bubble for a few seconds and remove from heat. Blend the mixture in the food processor. When the paste has cooled a little, blend in the rest of the butter and brandy. Pour into the little moulds and refrigerate when cool.

Pork and Spinach Pâté

1 kg (2 lb) spinach leaves, cooked
1 kg (2 lb) minced pork
300 g (10 oz) minced bacon
2 teaspoons Aromatic Salt
  (page 24)
2 teaspoons thyme
2 tablespoons white wine
$^1/_2$ teaspoon salt
1 teaspoon pepper
3 bacon rashers

*S*queeze the water out of the spinach and chop finely. Mix all the ingredients together well except for the bacon. Press the mixture into the terrine dish and smooth the top. Line the top with the bacon, in criss-cross fashion if liked, as in the picture opposite. Cover the terrine and put into a baking dish of hot water. Bake in a preheated oven at 180°C (350°F) for 1¹/₂ hours. Test with a skewer. Weight the terrine and re-frigerate when cold.

Salted and Brined Meats

*P*ork and beef have been preserved for thousands of years with salt and brine solutions. Before refrigeration, meat was kept in large glazed tubs, crocks and pots filled with brine. Meats could be kept for 4 or 5 weeks before being taken out for cooking, or for smoking to preserve them even longer. I suggest you consider salting and brining joints of meat to enhance the flavour more than to preserve. Though you can buy a pumped leg of pork or lamb from the butcher, you will find that a hot, homemade joint of salt pork will be a real culinary delight. With careful planning, the actual time spent on making these treats is not very long at all. It is handy to have a joint of meat in the brine crock for unexpected visitors to share the joy of such homely tasty food.

I always use sea salt for salting or brining—you will find you achieve a much better flavour. Never use table running salt,

Pork and Spinach Pâté (page 133) makes a simple but rich picnic lunch, accompanied by Pickled Onions (page 65), marinated black olives and crusty bread, washed down with some wine. Plaiting the top bacon makes an attractive finish to the pâté.

as that has chemicals in it. If you don't have a crock, a spotlessly clean, large china bowl will do. You need a piece of wood for a lid to keep the meat below the surface. Saltpetre can be bought from a butcher or chemist—it keeps the meat pink. Spices and herbs are added to improve the flavour. Sugar counteracts the hardening effects of salt. Everything must be spotlessly clean when preserving.

Even joints of fresh meat will improve by a soak in the brine for 12 hours. The salting time for brined meats depends on the size of the joint. I suggest you brine for no longer than 2 weeks. If white mould begins to float on the surface, remove the meat and renew the brine, scrubbing everything clean again. The meat will still be all right, but discard it if ever in any doubt. Take meat out with clean tongs so you don't run the risk of introducing bacteria into the brine. Keep the crock in a cool place.

Meats suitable for salting are:
Pork: the leg, shoulder and loin, hock, belly, trotters. Brine for 3 to 12 days.
Beef: silverside and brisket. Brine for 7 to 12 days.
Lamb: shoulder, leg and loin. Brine for 7 to 12 days.
Duck: giblets removed. Brine for 1 to 2 days.

Brined Meats

This brine solution will be right for whatever joint of meat you select. The table above gives you the time to allow for brining. Also try the Aromatic Salt (page 24) for a change. Cook the meats as for the Hand of Pickled Pork (page 136).

14 cups (6 imp. pts) water,
preferably filtered
3 cups (1¹/₂ lb) sea salt
3 cups (1 lb) brown sugar
¹/₄ cup (2 oz) saltpetre
1 tablespoon Flavoured Salt for
Salting Meat (page 24).

*P*ut the ingredients into a pan and bring to the boil. Boil for 10 minutes and pour, strained, into the meticulously clean crock. When cold, put in the meat or meats. Put the sterilised board on top and hold it down with a weight. When you remove a piece of meat you also remove salt, so you may want to add more brine. Make some as above and add to crock when cold.

*H*and of *P*ickled *P*ork

If you haven't eaten a hand (shoulder) of pickled pork, you are in for a big treat. It tastes as good as the leg but, I think, is more tender and has the bonus of being much cheaper. I also use pork cooked as below to make Jellied Parsley Pork (page 137) as a special party or picnic dish. If you haven't time to brine, buy the hand already brined from the butcher. This recipe makes a grand dinner for family or friends. Serve with Sauce Tartare (page 32), Green Sauce (page 38), Cumberland Sauce (page 41) or Horseradish Mustard (page 36).

Hand of pickled pork
1 onion
1 leek
1 carrot
1 orange, halved
Bouquet Garni (page 88)
1 tablespoon Quatre-Epices
(page 43) or Spezie all'Italiana
(page 43)
1 tablespoon chopped ginger

*R*inse the pork and place in the pan with the rest of the ingredients. Cover

with cold water and slowly bring to the boil. Simmer for 3 to 4 hours. Serves 8.

If you like salty vegetables you could simmer your vegetables in with the meat. Otherwise, cook them separately in chicken stock. Suitable vegetables are carrots, potatoes, turnips, cabbage, parsnips, onions and leeks. This dish is rather like a pot au feu. You serve the meat on a large carving dish surrounded by the vegetables. Some pickled fruits (Chapter 3) could be placed on the table. Don't throw the pork stock away —reduce it and freeze ready to cook split peas, beans or lentils.

*D*ry *S*alt *M*eat

Use the same meats as for Brined Meats (page 135). For 3 kg (6 lb) of meat you need the following amount:

2 cups (1 lb) salt
3 tablespoons saltpetre
¹/₄ cup (2 oz) Flavoured Salt for
Salting Meat (page 24)

*M*ix the ingredients together. Put ¹/₂ cup of salt mixture in the bottom of the preserving pot. Rub the rest into the flesh of the meat. Lay the meat on the salt, skin side up. Pack any leftover salt around the meat. Cover with a lid. After a few days the meat juices turn the salt to brine. The meat will last in salt for about a month. Cook it the same way as Hand of Pickled Pork (this page) or try my version of jambon persillé (see next recipe).

Jellied Parsleyed Pork

1.5 kg (3 lb) pickled pork or
cooked ham
2 cups (18 fl oz) chicken stock
2 cups (18 fl oz) dry white wine
Pepper
6 juniper berries
1 cup finely chopped parsley
1 tablespoon capers
¹/₃ cup chopped chives
2¹/₂ tablespoons gelatine
2 tablespoons white wine vinegar

Cut the pork into cubes as you cut it off the bone. Put the stock and wine into a saucepan and bring to the boil. Add the pork, some pepper and the juniper berries and simmer for 5 minutes. Take the pork out and reserve the hot liquid. Put the pieces into a bowl or a terrine dish and add parsley, capers and chives layer by layer. Soften the gelatine in a little cold water and then stir into the hot liquid. When it is dissolved, allow the liquid to cool. Add the vinegar and pour over the pork. Let it set in the refrigerator. To serve, unmould from the bowl or serve it in the terrine dish. Serve with Hot Honey Mustard (page 26) and Creamed Horseradish Sauce (page 36).

Potted Tongue

Another delicious old-fashioned dish now out of favour. A brined tongue is one of the cheapest meats to buy; it hasn't much fat and is, I believe, impossible to ruin. Cook the tongue the same way as Hand of Pickled Pork (opposite page).

1 brined and cooked tongue (about
750 g [1¹/₂ lb])
1 cup (7 oz) Clarified Butter
(page 21)
1 teaspoon Quatre-Epices (page 43)

Peel the tongue and chop it up. Blend it to a paste with the butter and spices in the food processor. Pack into small porcelain soufflé dishes. Pour extra clarified butter over the top to seal if you want to keep them longer. Refrigerate. Makes about 4 small dishes.

Confit (Preserved Meats and Poultry)

An old method of preserving meat, this is still interesting today as it gives the meats a different flavour. It is an old-fashioned meal-in-a-minute. Just take a piece of meat out of its preserving jar to eat cold or heat up in a frying pan with garlic and herbs and serve with sauté potatoes. It is traditionally added to cassoulet, a mixture of baked haricot beans and meats. Add to White Bean Soup (page 122) for a meal fit for a king.

For preserving, duck, chicken, goose or rabbit should be jointed but not boned, and pork should be cut from the loin into pieces big enough for two people.

Preserving 2 kg (4 lb) of Meat

¹/₂ cup (4 oz) salt
1 teaspoon saltpetre
2 tablespoons Aromatic Salt
(page 24)
Best quality lard, goose or duck fat,
half the weight of the meat.

Mix the salts together, then rub all over the meat and leave to salt for a day. Put the lard into a large pan and melt. Add the meat and cook slowly for 1¹/₂ to 2 hours. Test with a skewer —when ready, no juices will flow out.

Allow lard to cool so it doesn't crack the preserving jars.

I use large preserving jars, but traditionally stoneware and glazed earthenware pots with wooden tops were used. If you have one, be sure to sterilise it well (see Chapter 1). Pour some of the strained lard into the bottom of the sterilised jar, pack in the pieces of meat, leaving room for a layer of lard to enclose the meat (about half the depth of your little finger). Pour the lard over— right up to the brim as it will contract as it cools. When cool, seal the jars. Keep in a cool, dark, airy place. It will keep for 6 months untouched, but refrigerate once opened. Always keep the remaining pieces covered with lard when you take a piece out.

Pork Rillettes

This recipe can be used for duck, goose, chicken or rabbit. Serve as a starter with toast or crusty bread.

500 g (1 lb) belly of pork, treated for 24 hours with Confit salts (page 137)
¼ cup (2 oz) good lard

Cut the meat into bite-size pieces. Put the lard in a pan and very gently brown the pork. Pour off the lard and reserve. Cover the pan and cook the pork for 4 hours. Put in more lard if it begins to stick. When the meat is cooked, shred it, using 2 forks. Pack the pork into sterilised jars and pour the well-sieved fat over it. There should be a layer of lard as thick as your thumb over the top of the pork. Seal well. It will last for months in the pantry.

Sausages

I think every cuisine in the world has its own varieties of sausage—the well-known salamis of Italy, the meaty sausages from France such as Toulouse sausage, merguez from the Middle East and, of course, the frankfurter and bratwurst sausages from Germany. There is no end to the variety, so experiment with flavourings as I do. Always buy top quality mince from the butcher or make your own in the food processor.

A sausage is basically a harmonious blend of meat, fat and flavourings. The more fat, the longer it will keep. If, like me, you don't eat fat or fatty meats, add an onion instead to keep the sausage moist. If you don't want to go to the bother of making sausages, use the blends to make rissoles.

Wrap the sausages in crépinette (caul), or you can wrap them in muslin and gently simmer. If you have a cool, dark, airy cellar, you can try drying the sausages. As I live in a rather hot, humid climate, I prefer to freeze the sausages I'm not going to use within 5 days. I find sausages freeze very well. You could also preserve them in lard the same way as for Confit (page 137).

Sausages are easy to make once you get the knack of pushing the meat into the sausage skins. Call in a friend to help the first time. Buy the skins from your butcher and keep in salt in the fridge. When you are making sausages, soak the skins in warm water for several hours and run water through the skins to open them up and make it easier to force the meat in. Just put one end in the tap. You must have a sausage funnel.

Duck Confit (page 137) being removed from its storage jar to make White Bean Soup (page 122). The meat is first marinated in a spicy salt brine then roasted and reserved in lard. Wash the lard off with hot water if you are on a fat-free diet.

To make sausages. Mix all the ingredients together thoroughly in a bowl. Knot one end of the sausage skin and tie the other to the funnel and ram in the meat mixture, or use a sausage-filling machine. Twist the sausage into links. Using a large sewing needle, prick the sausages all over to let the air escape. Knot the other end and hang up for 12 to 24 hours—if it isn't too hot a day, in which case, refrigerate.

Toulouse Sausage

For a special treat cook these as for Sausages in Tomato Sauce (page 142).

750 g (1¹/₂ lb) lean pork
250 g (¹/₂ lb) hard back fat
1 teaspoon salt
¹/₂ teaspoon saltpetre
1 teaspoon Quatre-Epices (page 43)
Thin sausage casings, soaked

Minced meat is too fine for this recipe. You must coarsely chop it yourself. Make sausages by the method described above. Serves 6.

Chinese White Sausage

¹/₄ cup (2 oz) dried Chinese mushrooms, soaked and finely chopped
500 g (1 lb) chicken meat, minced
500 g (1 lb) lean pork, minced
1 teaspoon salt
1 teaspoon Five-Spice Salt (page 24)
¹/₄ teaspoon chilli powder
2 tablespoons Chinese wine or dry sherry
2 tablespoons light soy sauce
Thick sausage casings, soaked

Make sausages by the method described above. Serves 6.

Large Boiling Sausage

Buy skins of the large intestine for this sausage which tastes great boiled with root vegetables and served with Horseradish Mustard (page 36).

1 kg (2 lb) lean pork mince
250 g (¹/₂ lb) pork belly, minced
1 teaspoon salt
1 teaspoon pepper
1 teaspoon Quatre-Epices (page 43)
¹/₄ teaspoon cayenne
1/₂ teaspoon saltpetre
1 tablespoon brandy
3 garlic cloves, chopped
Thick sausage casings, soaked

Make sausages by the method described above left. Serves 10.

Boudin Blanc (White Sausage)

A delicious change from the hearty red meats. These will taste delicious cooked with grapes, see recipe page 142.

500 g (1 lb) raw chicken meat, minced
500 g (1 lb) lean pork, minced
500 g (1 lb) belly pork, minced
1 onion, minced
1 cup (9 fl oz) light cream
1 cup (2 oz) soft breadcrumbs
1 tablespoon chopped thyme
3 eggwhites
1 teaspoon salt
1 teaspoon Quatre-Epices (page 43)
Thin sausage casings, soaked

Make sausages by the method described above left. Serves 10 to 12.

Thai Pork Sausage

*I hope you are beginning to appreciate the
benefits of having all your spices and pastes
already made up in your pantry. Enjoy that
inner glow of satisfaction.*

> *1 kg (2 lb) lean pork, minced*
> *250 g ($^1/_2$ lb) pork belly, minced*
> *1 teaspoon salt*
> *1 onion, finely chopped*
> *$^1/_2$ cup coriander, chopped*
> *2 tablespoons Thai Green Curry
> Paste (page 50)*
> *3 tablespoons thick Coconut Milk
> (page 25)*
> *Thin sausage casings, soaked*

Make sausages by the method described on the opposite page. Serves 6.

Merguez Sausages

*Barbecue and serve with Spicy Tomato
Sauce (page 34) in pita bread. And watch
out—they are fiery!*

> *1 kg (2 lb) lean beef, minced*
> *90 g (3 oz) beef fat, finely chopped*
> *4 garlic cloves, chopped*
> *3 tablespoons red wine*
> *1 teaspoon salt*
> *1 teaspoon saltpetre*
> *1 teaspoon pepper*
> *2 teaspoons Harissa (page 54)*
> *Thin sausage casings, soaked*

Make sausages by the method described on the opposite page. Serves 6.

Bratwurst Sausages

*Serve with Horseradish Mustard (page
36) and dark rye bread, some Pickled
Gherkins (page 71) or Onions (page 65),
and wash it down with beer and schnapps.
The Germans, like the French, make the*

*most delectable meaty sausages. My hus-
band and I have enjoyed sausage tastings in
Hamburg at a shop devoted entirely to
sausages where you can choose from hundreds
of varieties.*

> *1 kg (2 lb) lean pork, minced*
> *250 g ($^1/_2$ lb) belly pork, minced*
> *2 teaspoons salt*
> *1 teaspoon saltpetre*
> *3 teaspoons pepper*
> *$^1/_2$ cup chopped herbs (thyme,
> rosemary and sage)*
> *Thin sausage casings, soaked*

Make sausages by the method described on the opposite page. Serves 6.

Hungarian Sausages

*Grill or barbecue these sausages and eat with
red cabbage or sauerkraut.*

> *500 g (1 lb) veal, minced*
> *500 g (1 lb) lean pork, minced*
> *2 eggs*
> *2 garlic cloves, minced*
> *1 onion, minced*
> *1 teaspoon salt*
> *1 teaspoon saltpetre*
> *1 tablespoon paprika*
> *2 tablespoons chopped marjoram*
> *12 tablespoons chopped parsley*
> *Thin sausage casings, soaked*

Make sausages by the method described on the opposite page. Serves 4.

Chilli Lamb Sausage

I find the meat from the shoulder of lamb best for sausages. It is sweet and very tender and has enough fat in it naturally—though, for myself, I trim it off.

>   1 kg (2 lb) lamb, minced
>   4 chillies, finely chopped
>   1 onion, finely chopped
>   2 garlic cloves, finely chopped
>   2 tablespoons finely chopped mint
>   3 teaspoons caraway seeds
>   1 teaspoon salt
>   1 teaspoon saltpetre
>   1 teaspoon pepper
>   1 egg
>   Thin sausage casings, soaked

*M*ake sausages by the method described on page 140. Serves 4.

Cooking Sausages

Of course there are even more ways of cooking sausages than there are sausages. Here are some of my favourite ways other than barbecuing or grilling.

Sausages in Tomato Sauce

It is not always necessary to link sausages when you make them. Cook them in a ring, like a coil of rope. It looks spectacular on a dish or the barbecue. Have fun trying this recipe with different kinds of sausages.

>   1 tablespoon olive oil
>   20 pickling onions or shallots
>   1 metre (1 yard) of sausage
>   2 cups (18 fl oz) Fresh Tomato
>   Sauce (page 32)
>   1 teaspoon salt
>   1 teaspoon pepper

*P*ut the oil in the pan and cook the onions. Remove and keep warm. Put the sausages into the pan and cook for about 15 minutes or until nearly done. Add the Fresh Tomato Sauce and season and put the onions back in. If you have an attractive pan, serve it in the pan at the table. Serves 6.

Sausage with Grapes

Put some extra links into the sausages so they are only the length of your little finger. This is a wonderful combination of spicy meat and warm sweet grapes. Perfect for lunch in the garden on a spring day.

> $1^1/_2$ tablespoons olive oil
>   12 Toulouse Sausages (page 140)
> $^1/_2$ cup (4 fl oz) dry white wine
>   1 kg (2 lb) seedless green grapes,
>   stalks removed

*H*eat the oil in the pan and then brown the sausages all over and cook for about another 10 minutes. Remove from pan and pour off the oil. Return sausages to pan with the wine and grapes. Cook over a high heat for 5 minutes and serve. Serves 6.

Toulouse Sausages (page 140) cooked with wine and seedless green grapes—a really delicious combination. Serve with crusty bread and a tomato salad.

Cured Fish

Gravlaks (Salt-Cured Salmon)

An ancient Scandinavian way to preserve raw fish. Trout is also excellent made this way. If you do not want to cure a whole fish, the tail end or middle piece will be just as good. Ask your fishmonger to fillet the salmon for you. Weigh the fillets and use the same proportion of fish to salt and sugar. Serve thinly sliced with rye bread and butter.

1.5 kg (3 lb) salmon, in 2 fillets
1 tablespoon aquavit or flavourless
   vodka
2 teaspoons sugar
4$^1/_2$ teaspoons salt
1 teaspoon pepper
1 cup freshly chopped dill

*W*ipe the fish fillets clean with a kitchen paper towel. Sprinkle the aquavit over the fillets. Mix the sugar, salt, pepper and dill together and gently rub the fillets with it. Put one fillet skin-side down on a cold, sterilised dish. Place the other fillet on top of the first, skin-side up. If there is any flavouring left, put it between the fillets. Cover the salmon plate with aluminium foil and put a weight on top. Store in the refrigerator in the warmest section. Turn the fillets twice a day. Pour the pressed-out liquid back between the fillets. You can remove the weights after 2 days. The gravlaks will be ready in 4 days. Cut in thin slices. Serve with thinly sliced rye bread and freshly chopped dill or with a dill sauce. Make a Vinaigrette (page 19) and add 2 tablespoons of chopped dill. Serves 8 to 10.

Brined Trout

A simpler way to brine trout and salmon and very tasty. Serve with capers, radishes and unsalted butter as well as rye bread, of course. Garnish with chopped dill and lemon wedges.

$^1/_2$ cup (4 oz) sea salt
4 cups (1$^3/_4$ imp. pts) water
1 kg (2 lb) trout fillets

*B*oil the salt and water and allow to cool. Put the fish and brine in a bowl, cover and leave in the refrigerator for 2 days. Drain and dry the fish, and slice thinly to serve. Serves 4 to 6.

Taramasalata

This is a dip made from the salted and dried roe of grey mullet, called Tarama in Greek. Although I'm not recommending you preserve this, it is a very handy food to have in the kitchen and can quickly be transformed into Taramasalata. Serve with crusty bread or flat bread.

125 g (4 oz) tarama or smoked
   cod's roe, skinned
Juice of 2 lemons
$^1/_2$ cup (2 oz) soft breadcrumbs
$^1/_4$ teaspoon cayenne
3 tablespoons olive oil
1 spring onion, finely chopped on
   the slant

*P*ut the roe, lemon, bread and cayenne into the food processor and blend. Slowly add the oil until it is the consistency of mayonnaise. Garnish with spring onion. Serves 4 to 6.

Whole Roast Garlic in Oil (page 73). A delicious stand-by for an alfresco meal to serve with cold meats, cheese and salad. They look so beautiful it can sometimes be hard to open the bottle.

Bagna Carda

This hot garlic and anchovy dip is another handy starter that can be made in next to no time from your pantry. Serve it with a platter of raw vegetables and bread for people to dip into the hot fishy sauce. Choose from these vegetables—capsicums (peppers), carrots, cauliflower, broccoli, mushrooms, spring onions, boiled potatoes, celery, beans, fennel, asparagus and artichoke hearts.

1 cup (9 fl oz) olive oil
6 garlic cloves, crushed
14 anchovies, drained and chopped
$^1/_2$ cup (4 oz) butter

Put the oil in the pan and add the garlic. Cook until it is tender but do not brown it. Add the anchovies and simmer, stirring until the anchovies dissolve. Add the butter and stir. It is ready as soon as the butter is dissolved. Keep it warm on a spirit stove. Serves 8 as a starter.

Cheese and Yoghurt

Soft cheese is made from curds that have been drained—for hard cheese, they must be fermented as well. Cheese is produced by coagulation which occurs with the addition of a curdling agent, most often rennet (junket tablets). For soft cheese, the curds are cut up in large pieces and put in moulds or hung up in muslin to drain further. Curds for hard cheese are put in moulds or baskets and pressed with weights. This is when fermentation begins.

I have always enjoyed making my own fresh cheese. It isn't difficult to make and I like experimenting with added spices and herbs. I think it satisfies that deep feeling of the miraculous nature of cooking—transforming milk into cheese, or eggs and oil into mayonnaise. It continues to be a basic rewarding pleasure.

Fresh Cheese with Herbs

4 junket tablets (rennet)
6 cups (2$^3/_4$ imp. pts) goat's milk or cow's milk
2 cups (18 fl oz) thick cream
$^1/_2$ cup (4 fl oz) buttermilk
1 teaspoon salt

Dissolve the junket tablets in a little cold water. Bring the milk, cream and buttermilk to blood heat (37°C; 98°F) in a saucepan, then remove from the heat. Stir in the rennet and leave to set in a warm place. (I get good results on top of the water heater.) The curd will form and separate from the whey in an hour or more. Put the curds into a cheese mould and refrigerate for a day or two, or wrap the curds up in 3 layers of muslin and tie up as a ball. Suspend it over a bowl to catch the drips. Leave hanging for 12 hours and you have a nice soft cheese. If you want it firmer, keep in the refrigerator for several days. Work in the salt, then decide in which of the following ways you would like to flavour it.

Herbed Cheese
Roll the cheese into balls then roll in a mixture of herbs—1 tablespoon each of finely chopped savory, thyme and marjoram.

Paprika Cheese
To serve with drinks. Roll the cheese into small balls and roll in 2 tablespoons paprika and fennel seeds.

Tapénade Cheese

Add a ¹/₂ cup of Tapénade or Green Olive Paste (page 77) to the cheese. Form into balls and roll in 2 tablespoons thyme and pepper. Serve with fresh crusty bread as a starter.

Cumin Cheese

Roll balls of the cheese over whole cumin seeds. Great starter while you stand around the barbecue waiting for the sausages to cook.

Fruity Cheese

To serve at the end of a dinner party. To the cheese add 1 tablespoon each of chopped dried apricots, peaches and apples and 2 tablespoons chopped pistachio nuts. Mix well and form into a mould by laying muslin over a sieve. Press the cheese into it and smooth the top. Refrigerate for a few hours.

Almond Cheese Dessert

To the basic fresh cheese add 2 tablespoons of Vanilla Caster Sugar (page 4) and ¹/₂ cup freshly toasted almonds. Serve with one of your fruit desserts, such as Peaches in Brandy (page 97).

Marinated Fresh Cheese

You can prolong the life of your fresh goat or cow's milk cheese by marinating it in olive oil with herbs to flavour. The oil and herbs intensify the flavour of the cheese. It's wise to keep this refrigerated if you live in a hot climate. You can buy goat fetta cheese and marinate it the same way for a quick and easy starter. Serve with vine-ripened tomato slices, a few marinated olives and crusty bread and you have a starter fit for the gods. Use the oil for cooking.

Roll your fresh cheese into small balls or scoops and pack into cooled sterilised preserving jars. Add all or some of the following flavours:

2 garlic cloves
4 red chillies
1 teaspoon pepper
3 sprigs thyme or rosemary
4 bay leaves
Olive oil to cover

*P*our virgin olive oil over to cover, seal and refrigerate. Ready to eat in a week if you can wait that long.

Fromage Fort

This is a preserved cheese to make from some matured goat's cheese and eau de vie. You need a straight-sided stoneware pot, similar to a stilton pot. The cheese will last for years like this—just top it up every now and then. Serve as a starter from the pot for guests to help themselves.

250 g (8 oz) mature goat's cheese
250 g (8 oz) fresh goat's cheese
1 teaspoon chopped thyme
¹/₂ teaspoon salt
¹/₂ teaspoon pepper
2 tablespoons eau de vie or brandy
1 tablespoon olive oil

*P*ut all the ingredients except for eau de vie and oil in a bowl and blend gradually, adding the eau de vie and oil as needed. Stop as soon as it has the consistency of fresh cheese. Pack the cheese into the sterilised pot and cover. Store in a cold place or refrigerate.

*H*omemade *Yoghurt*

Yoghurt is gradually becoming an essential ingredient in cooking as its health value is being recognised. It is a wonderful source of calcium for those like myself who don't like milk. I use it as the cooking medium for most of my curries. It's a good idea to make your own if you use it a lot. Make sure the yoghurt you start off with is a natural cultured yoghurt and not flavoured. You need a vacuum flask with a wide neck for the yoghurt to set in. This makes it a foolproof method, I think. If you do not have a vacuum flask, keep it in a lidded container, cover and leave in a warm place, wrapped in a towel to keep the warmth in. Or leave for a day in a sunny place.

> 2 cups (18 fl oz) goat's or cow's
>   milk
> 1¹/₂ tablespoons yoghurt

*P*ut the milk in a pan and bring just to the boil; lower the heat and allow to cool to blood temperature. Remove any skin that may have formed on the surface. Lightly whisk in the live yoghurt. Pour it into a vacuum flask and screw down the lid. Let it stand for 10 to 12 hours. Refrigerate. It should last for a week. Get into the rhythm of making some every week. To get a thicker texture add a tablespoon of powdered skimmed milk with the live yoghurt.

*L*abna

*T*he next step, once you have mastered yoghurt making, is to make Labna yoghurt cheese. All you do is mix in a teaspoon of salt for every 2 cups of yoghurt. Put the yoghurt in 3 layers of muslin and hang up for 4 to 5 hours over a bowl to catch the whey. I recommend starting with 4 cups of yoghurt and 2 teaspoons of salt. Then put the cheese in a cheese mould or press it into a sieve with a layer of cheesecloth over it. Smooth the top, then up-end it on a plate. It makes a good shape. Decorate with herbs and spices and pour a little olive oil over just before serving. Use the same flavourings as for Fresh Cheese (page 146). You can also roll it into balls and marinate in olive oil as for Marinated Fresh Cheese (page 147).

*M*inty *Yoghurt Dip*

I just love this refreshing dip. Serve it with pita bread and raw vegetables. I even use it as a sauce with steamed vegetables. Sometimes I add a little Harissa (page 54) to it.

> 1 cup (7 oz) cottage cheese
> 1 cup (7 oz) yoghurt
> ¹/₄ cup mint leaves, finely chopped
> 2 garlic cloves, finely chopped
> 2 tablespoons chopped chives
> Juice of ¹/₂ lemon
> 1 teaspoon pepper

*P*ut all the ingredients into the food processor and blend to a thick, smooth sauce. Add a little more lemon juice if it is too thick. Refrigerate until needed.

Pizzas

*O*riginally a piece of Italian flat bread covered with a few savoury things like anchovy, mozzarella, onions, olives and, later on, slices of tomato. Nowadays, there doesn't seem to be anything you can't put on a pizza. As always, homemade is best. Keep some of this dough in the freezer and make your own instant pizzas. Freeze

The secret of Pizza with Tomatoes and Olives (page 150) and its sweet taste is to cook the onions until they are reduced and beginning to turn brown and mushy. Keep the lid on the pan while cooking them.

before leaving to rise. Practise restraint with the flavourings. Make individual pizzas for a change. You'll feed 4 with this recipe, depending on how big your appetites are.

Pizza with Tomatoes and Olives

Bread dough
2 cups (8 oz) flour, sifted
1 teaspoon salt
1 teaspoon sugar
7 g (¹/₄ oz) dry yeast
³/₄ cup (7 fl oz) warm water
3 tablespoons olive oil
Filling
2 tablespoons olive oil
4 onions, finely sliced
2 garlic cloves, chopped
1 cup (9 fl oz) Fresh Tomato Sauce (page 32)
1 tablespoon chopped rosemary
1 teaspoon pepper
¹/₂ teaspoon salt
1 cup (5 oz) sliced mozzarella cheese
6 anchovy fillets
20 black olives, pitted and quartered
1 tablespoon oregano to garnish

To make the dough, put the flour, salt and sugar into a bowl. Mix the yeast with the warm water. Make a well in the flour and pour in the yeast mixture and olive oil. Knead to a dough until it is light and elastic. Shape it into a ball, cover with a floured tea-towel and leave in a warm place for an hour. It will double its size.

Heat the oil and cook the onions. Add the garlic and tomato sauce and season. Cook 5 more minutes. When the pizza dough is ready, pat it into a circle or a square. Cover it with the onion and tomato mixture. Arrange the cheese over the top and decorate with the anchovy and olives. Sprinkle with oregano. Bake in a preheated oven 230°C (450°F) for 20 to 25 minutes. Serves 6.

Pizza with Prosciutto
Slice ripe tomatoes over base of pizza. Cover with slices of mozzarella and thin slices of prosciutto. Sprinkle with rosemary, pepper and salt and parmesan.

Pizza with Onions
Cook 6 onions, finely sliced, in 2 tablespoons of olive oil and then simmer in a little milk. Spread thickly over the base and add pitted olives.

Pizza with Sun-Dried Tomatoes
First of all, spoon a layer of Fresh Tomato Sauce (page 32) over the base. Then spread 1 cup (2 oz) of Sun-Dried Tomatoes in Oil (page 88) over. Add ¹/₂ cup of chopped basil leaves, 1¹/₂ tablespoons of capers and pitted olives. Lay slices of mozzarella over and bake.

Pizza with Merguez
Coat the pizza base with Fresh Tomato Sauce (page 32), add thick slices of cooked Merguez Sausages (page 141), sprinkle with chopped spring onions and capsicum (pepper) strips. Sprinkle with Chilli Sauce (page 38), add slices of mozzarella and bake.

Savoury Flans

Once you have mastered pastry making, or if you have some frozen pastry at hand, it's very easy to make these savoury flans. They always seem to be a special treat for a picnic or a party. Experiment with the fillings. Look in the store cupboard—perhaps some dried mushrooms would go well instead of spinach. There are endless variations.

Pâte Brisée

$1^3/_4$ cups (7 oz) flour, sifted
125 g (4 oz) butter, softened
1 egg yolk
$^1/_4$ teaspoon salt
2 teaspoons iced water
Lemon juice
Eggwash (beaten egg yolk)

Put the flour and butter into a bowl and rub them together with your fingers until the butter is completely absorbed and the texture resembles breadcrumbs. Mix the egg with the salt, water and lemon juice and add to the flour. Stir it around and then mix with your fingers until you have a ball. Add more moisture if it gets too dry. Put the pastry on a floured surface and knead it lightly with the palms of your hands until it is smooth. Wrap in plastic and refrigerate for half an hour or up to 3 days. (Or it can be frozen.) Put the dough on a floured surface and roll out with a floured rolling pin. Line the flan tin and refrigerate again before baking and filling. Cook in a preheated oven 230°C (450°F) for 30 to 40 minutes. Makes 20 to 23 cm (8 to 9 in.) flan ring.

Onion Flan

If you don't have any of your fresh cheese handy, blend $^1/_2$ cup yoghurt and 1 cup low-fat ricotta cheese in the food processor.

6 onions, sliced
2 tablespoons oil
2 eggs
$^1/_2$ cup (3 oz) Fresh Cheese
    (page 146)
$^1/_2$ cup (4 fl oz) thick cream
1 teaspoon salt
1 teaspoon pepper
1 tablespoon caraway seeds
1 quantity Pâte Brisée (this page)

Cook the onions in the oil until they are very soft. Beat the eggs into the fresh cheese and cream, and season. Put in the onions and mix well. Roll out the dough on a floured surface. Line a 20 to 23 cm (8 to 9 in.) flan ring and pinch up the edge to form a raised border to contain the filling. Pour in the cheese and onion mixture and bake in a preheated oven 230°C (450°F) for 30 to 40 minutes. Serves 6.

Spinach and Ham Quiche

1 tablespoon butter
1 slice ham, diced
2 egg yolks
$^1/_2$ cup (4 fl oz) thick cream
$^1/_2$ cup ($2^1/_2$ oz) grated gruyère
    cheese
1 teaspoon salt
1 teaspoon pepper
1 teaspoon nutmeg
$1^1/_2$ cups cooked, drained and
    chopped spinach

Heat the butter and cook the ham until golden. Drain on absorbent kitchen paper. Combine the egg yolks and cream and mix well. Add the cheese, and season. Stir in the ham. Roll out the dough and line the flan ring. Spread the spinach over the bottom of it. Pour the egg and ham mixture over it. Bake for 30 to 40 minutes. Serves 6.

Ham and Garlic Flan
Substitute 30 garlic cloves, peeled, for the spinach. Remember garlic isn't as pungent when cooked.

Ham and Tomato Flan
Substitute a punnet of cherry tomatoes for the spinach.

151

6 Sweet Things

*O*ld-fashioned bread and butter pudding, prune and almond tart, pawpaw sorbet, watermelon granita, chocolate ice-cream, strawberry parfait, black treacle cake, and chocolate walnut rocks—all are deliciously wicked treats for ending a perfect meal. They can be made with stored items such as stale bread and dried fruits or be packed ready in the freezer, or lying in airtight tins ready for you to decide on the occasion to serve them. Never forget to label or you may be in for some amazing culinary disasters.

Apple and Blueberry Pie (page 158) taken straight from the oven to the table. The casual, crusted look of the top says it's homemade—and good for you.

Place the pudding in a baking dish with hot water coming half-way up the sides of the soufflé dish. Bake in a preheated oven 160°C (325°F) for 50 minutes or until the custard has risen and is firm and crusty on top. Serves 8.

Puddings

There are desserts scattered throughout this book as well as in this chapter, so look up the index for a greater choice. Most of these are very old recipes that I have rewritten for today's lighter tastes. They are all made from ingredients from the pantry with the addition of some fresh ingredients from time to time.

Bread and Butter Pudding

A heavenly dessert—and terribly simple to make once you have mastered the art of making a custard.

> 12 slices of stale fruit bread, crusts removed
> $^1/_4$ cup (2 oz) currants
> $^1/_4$ cup (2 oz) citrus peel, chopped
> 2 cups (18 fl oz) milk
> 3 eggs
> 1 egg yolk
> 1 tablespoon Vanilla Sugar (page 4)
> 3 tablespoons rum

Grease a china soufflé dish with butter. Arrange the bread slices in the dish, sprinkling the currants and citrus peel between the layers. To make the custard, put the milk over a low heat, mix together the eggs, egg yolk and sugar, and when small holes begin appearing around the edge of the milk, pour in some of the egg mixture and gently mix. Gradually mix in all the egg mixture. Pour the custard over the bread and butter. Leave for $^1/_2$ hour.

Plum Pudding

This is an old recipe. It is a large quantity, so you can make some smaller puddings as well for later on in the year. They will last the whole year in the refrigerator. I prefer the look of a pudding cooked in a basin; but if you prefer to cook in calico, make sure your calico is absolutely clean and sprinkle some flour over the area that will wrap around the pudding. Tie securely with string, leaving enough room for the pudding to expand.

> 3 cups (1 lb) sultanas
> 2 cups (12 oz) raisins
> 2 cups (12 oz) prunes, stoned
> $^1/_2$ cup (2 oz) dried figs
> 2 cups (10 oz) currants
> $^1/_2$ cup (3 oz) citrus peel
> 2 cooking apples, grated
> 2 tablespoons grated lemon peel
> 2 cups (18 fl oz) dark rum
> 1 cup (7 oz) butter
> 1 cup (5 oz) dark brown sugar
> 6 eggs
> 7 cups ($1^3/_4$ lb) day-old wholemeal breadcrumbs
> 4 tablespoons plain wholemeal flour
> 1 teaspoon ground allspice berries
> 1 teaspoon grated nutmeg
> $2^1/_2$ teaspoons ground cinnamon
> $^1/_4$ teaspoon cloves
> 2 teaspoons bicarbonate of soda
> 1 teaspoon salt

Chop up all the dried fruits and citrus peel, and place in a large bowl. Add the apple, lemon peel and rum. Mix well, cover and leave for a week to macerate. Beat the butter until fluffy, add the sugar and beat until the mixture is creamy. Add the eggs one at a time, beating well in between. Combine the cream mixture with the fruit and breadcrumbs. Sift the flour, spices, soda and salt and add to the pudding mixture. To ensure the pudding will turn out perfectly, double grease heatproof basins in the following way: melt a little butter and brush it over the entire surface of the basin, refrigerate for ten minutes and grease again, chill. Transfer the pudding mixture into the individual basins. Cover the top of each basin with two layers of aluminium foil and tie with string. Place each in a saucepan with boiling water halfway up the side of the basin. Steam for 6 hours. Keep checking the water level in case more is needed. Keep the aluminium cover on and store in the refrigerator. Before eating, reheat the same way for 2 hours. Serves 16.

Persian Rice Pudding

If you can get Italian arborio rice it will taste infinitely better.

> ¹/₄ teaspoon saffron
> ³/₄ cup (5 oz) arborio or short-grain
>   rice, washed
> 1 cup (7 oz) Vanilla Sugar
>   (page 4)
> 2 teaspoons lemon juice
> ¹/₂ cup (2 oz) slivered almonds
> 2 teaspoons ground cinnamon

D issolve the saffron in a little hot water. Put the rice in a pan and add 1¹/₂ cups of cold water and the saffron. Bring to the boil, cover and leave on the lowest heat for 25 minutes. Meanwhile, put the sugar, lemon juice and ¹/₄ cup of water into a pan and bring to

the boil. Keep simmering while the rice cooks and the liquid is absorbed. Put the lemon syrup into the rice and cook until the liquid is almost absorbed. Stir in the almonds and sprinkle with cinnamon after it has been poured into a serving bowl. Serves 6.

Fruit Tarts

T here is nothing so pleasant to end a meal with as a homemade fruit tart. Here are some recipes for very simple tarts. This rich, sweet shortcrust pastry, Pâte Brisée Sucrée, can be successfully kept in the freezer, so you can whip up a tart at little notice. The supermarkets have excellent frozen pastry these days so I suggest you buy in the puff pastry and fillo pastry. Once you have your pastry base, it is just a matter of arranging sliced fruits such as apricots and apple in a spiral pattern around the pastry. It is then baked and, finally, glazed with redcurrant or apricot jam glaze.

Rich Shortcrust Pastry

Use this pastry for dessert pies, tarts and quiches. Follow the instructions for Pâte Brisée (page 151), adding 3 teaspoons of caster sugar and a few drops of vanilla essence when putting in the liquid ingredients.

Apricot Glaze

Redcurrant jelly glaze can be made the same way. Spoon a thin layer of glaze over the fruit in the flan while the glaze and the tart are still hot.

> ¹/₄ cup (3 oz) Orange and Apricot
>   Jam (page 92)
> Juice of 1 lemon
> 3 tablespoons water

P ut the ingredients into a pan and stir until it boils.

Dried Apricot Tart

Cook the apricots for 20 minutes in boiling water and the juice of half a lemon.

1 quantity Rich Shortcrust Pastry
  (page 155)
1 cup (11 oz) apricot jam
500 g (1 lb) dried apricots, cooked
  and drained
1 quantity Apricot Glaze (page 155)

Roll out the pastry to fit a 20 to 23 cm (8 to 9 in.) flan ring. Chill for 15 minutes. Spread the pastry with the jam and cover with the apricots. Bake in a preheated oven 230°C (450°F) for 30 to 40 minutes. Glaze while still hot. Eat cold. Serves 6 to 8.
Variations: Use this same recipe for sliced apples and pears with redcurrant jam and glaze. Try dried peaches with peach jam and glaze—the possibilities are endless and delicious.

Prune Tart

This delicious tart, made quickly from your pre-prepared ingredients, offers a great opportunity to use your Prunes in Rum (page 100). The tart is baked 'blind', that is, the pastry shell is cooked before adding the filling. Here again you can experiment with the fruits in your pantry to make different flavours. It is easy once you master the method.

1 quantity Rich Shortcrust Pastry
  (page 155)
15 prunes
2 eggs
$^1/_2$ cup (4 oz) Vanilla Caster
  Sugar (page 4)
3 tablespoons ground almonds
2 tablespoons extra thick cream

Roll out the pastry to fit a 20 to 23 cm (8 to 9 in.) flan ring. Chill for 15

minutes. To bake blind, cut a circle of greaseproof paper a bit larger than the ring, prick the pastry with a fork and cover with the paper, then weight the paper down with dried beans so the pastry won't rise. Put the tart in a preheated oven 230°C (450°F) for 20 minutes. Remove the beans. Keep the beans in a jar to use again. Beat the eggs and sugar in a bowl until thick. Add the almonds and cream and combine well. Arrange the prunes around the flan and pour in the almond mixture. Bake in a preheated oven as before for 40 to 45 minutes or until golden brown.

Baked Blind Fruit Tarts
The tart crust was half cooked in the previous recipe. Another way to make a fruit tart is to bake it completely, then add fresh fruit and glaze. Cook the pastry for 30 to 40 minutes. Remove from oven. When cold, slice up fresh or preserved fruit. Spread a layer of jam on the pastry, then arrange the fruit on top.

Freezer Tip: Pastry. Double up the quantities when making pâte brisée or rich shortcrust pastry and either keep the extra pastry in ball form, wrapped in plastic, or keep an unfilled flan in the freezer for later use. Wrap it in a polythene bag and pack in a cardboard box. Will last 6 months. Thaw at room temperature for a few hours.

Simple iced fruit drinks, laced with gin if you like, ready to serve at the beginning of a summer luncheon. Granitas (page 159) are quick to make, consisting only of a sugar syrup and fruit purée crushed in the food processor just before serving.

Puff Pastry Fruit Tarts

Use commercial frozen puff pastry for this. Cut a square or a rectangle from rolled out puff pastry and place on a greased baking tray. Prick the centre of this layer with a fork to prevent the pastry rising. Cut strips of pastry 2.5 cm (1 in.) wide and put around the edges of the pastry. This makes a border which will rise and give the tart an edge. Stick the strips on by brushing with beaten egg; this is known as eggwash and may be used to glaze the pastry as well. Place thinly sliced fruit in the tart—apples, nectarines, apricots, pears, plums or peaches. Brush some jam on the base first if liked, then glaze when cooked. Cook the same way as for Dried Apricot Tart (page 156). Or you can bake blind and fill with strawberries or raspberries (see Baked Blind Fruit Tarts, page 156).

Apple and Blueberry Pie

A delicious pie to make with ingredients from the pantry. You can use dried or preserved fruit if fresh are not available. Just soften the dried fruit in water for 20 minutes first and then drain.

> 6 apples, peeled, cored and sliced,
>   in acidulated water
> 4 punnets of blueberries
> $^1/_2$ cup (4 oz) Vanilla Sugar
>   (page 4)
> 2 quantities Rich Shortcrust Pastry
>   (page 155)
> $^1/_4$ cup (4 oz) butter
> Sugar to garnish
> Eggwash

*P*ut the apples and blueberries in separate bowls and sprinkle with vanilla sugar. Roll out the pastry and line a greased pie dish with it, leaving

enough pastry to drape over the top later. Combine the fruits and spoon into the pie dish. Dot with butter and fold the excess pastry over the top, leaving a gap in the middle. Sprinkle with sugar and put into a preheated oven 225°C (440°F) for half an hour. Take out pie and brush with eggwash and bake for another 15 minutes or until golden brown. Serves 8.

Desserts from the Freezer

*T*he fastest dessert around—just open the freezer door. If you haven't time to make your own ice-cream, bought ones are sometimes excellent—just spoon over some of your preserved fruit such as Grapes in Armagnac (page 100) or Tamarillos in Raspberry Liqueur (page 98). Heaven, and it only takes 5 minutes from freezer to table.

Prune Whip

Make this with dried apricots or peaches for a change. Sprinkle chopped walnuts or almonds on the top instead of the prune.

> 1 Earl Grey tea bag
> 250 g (8 oz) dried prunes, stoned
> $^1/_3$ cup (3 oz) caster sugar
> 250 g (8 oz) Fresh Cheese (page
>   146) or Yoghurt (page 149)
> 3 teaspoons Vanilla Sugar
>   (page 4)
> $^2/_3$ cup (6 fl oz) thick cream
> 6 Prunes in Rum (page 100)

*P*ut the tea bag in a bowl and pour boiling water over. Soak the prunes for 12 hours. Drain and cook them for 20 minutes until tender and then blend in the food processor. Add the caster sugar and fresh cheese and blend. Separately, beat the vanilla sugar and cream until stiff. Fold the cream gently into the prune mixture in a bowl. Put the prune whip into an icing bag and fill sundae glasses. Keep in the freezer. When serving, put a prune in rum on top of each glass. Will keep for a week in the freezer. Serves 6.

Granitas

A most refreshing drink for hot summer days. Granitas are made almost the same way as sorbets but drunk straight after the first puréeing.

Watermelon Granita

500g (1 lb) watermelon, seeded and diced
1 cup (9 fl oz) sorbet syrup (right)
3 tablespoons gin, optional

Purée the watermelon in the food processor with the sorbet syrup. Put into a flat freezer tray. Freeze. When ready to drink, purée again, add the gin and pour into chilled glasses. Serve straight away. Serves 6.
Variations:

Orange or Lemon Granita
2 cups (18 fl oz) orange juice, juice of 1 lemon, 1 cup (9 fl oz) sorbet syrup, 2 tablespoons sugar. Make as above. Serves 6.

Apricot or Peach Granita
500 g (1 lb) ripe apricots (pitted), 1 cup (9 fl oz) sorbet syrup, juice of a lemon. Make as above. Serves 6.

Strawberry or Blackberry Granita
500 g (1 lb) strawberries (hulled), juice of a lemon, 1 cup (9 fl oz) sorbet syrup, 3 tablespoons gin or Strawberry Liqueur (page 104) (optional).

Sorbets

An ideal dessert to have ready in the freezer. Don't store too long as sorbets don't keep as well as ice-cream. If you have a sorbetière then your life was meant to be easy. My instructions are for those without—these sorbets will be grainier but still lovely and fresh. If you have a sorbetière, follow the manufacturer's instructions.
To make a sorbet. Have a *sorbet syrup* prepared and stored in the fridge. It is made by combining 1 kg (2 lb) sugar with 1 litre (1³/₄ pts) of water. Bring to the boil, dissolve the sugar and leave to cool. This syrup is added to puréed fruit and fruit juice as required. Too much sugar inhibits setting. Lemon juice is very often added. Pour into a flat freezer tray and freeze. When it is two-thirds set take it from the freezer and blend in the food processor. You can add alcohol or 2 stiffly beaten eggwhites at this stage. Return to freezer.

Rockmelon and Orange Sorbet

1 ripe rockmelon (cantaloupe), peeled, seeded and roughly chopped
1 cup (9 fl oz) sorbet syrup (above)
³/₄ cup (7 fl oz) orange juice
3 tablespoons Orange Liqueur (page 104)

Put the melon in the food processor and blend to a pulp. Pour into a bowl and add the sorbet syrup and orange juice. Mix well. Freeze and when it is almost set remove from freezer, add the orange liqueur and blend to a smooth purée. Put back into freezer. Serve warmed slightly, in glass bowls or glasses. Serves 6.

Variations: Follow the basic method for rockmelon and orange sorbet, using the following combinations:

Pawpaw Sorbet

750 g (1$^1/_2$ lb) ripe pawpaw (papaya), 1 cup (9 fl oz) sorbet syrup, $^1/_2$ cup (4 fl oz) orange juice, $^1/_2$ cup (4 fl oz) lime juice, 3 tablespoons white rum. Serves 6.

Mango Sorbet

750 g (1$^1/_2$ lb) mango, 1 cup (9 fl oz) sorbet syrup, $^1/_2$ cup (4 fl oz) orange juice, $^1/_2$ cup (4 fl oz) lemon juice. Serves 6.

Blackberry Sorbet

750 g (1$^1/_2$ lb) blackberries, 1 cup (9 fl oz) sorbet syrup, $^3/_4$ cup (7 fl oz) water, 3 tablespoons lemon juice, 2 stiffly beaten eggwhites. Add the eggwhites after the first freezing and after you have reduced the ice to a purée.

Peach or Apricot Sorbet

750 g (1$^1/_2$ lb) peaches or apricots, peeled and stoned, 1 cup (9 fl oz) sorbet syrup, $^3/_4$ cup (7 fl oz) water, 3 tablespoons Apricot Liqueur (page 103).

Pineapple Sorbet

1 large pineapple, 1 cup (9 fl oz) sorbet syrup, $^1/_2$ cup (4 fl oz) water, 3 tablespoons lemon juice, 3 tablespoons kirsch.

Ice-Creams

Ice-cream is the perfect dessert, especially when it is homemade and based on the classic Crème Anglaise custard—an egg custard made from cream and milk. It is rich and smooth perfection of which there is no equal. Ice-cream cannot be made really successfully without an ice-cream maker, however, because it needs to be churned to prevent ice crystals forming. So I'm not suggesting you try the beat and freeze method as for sorbets. Don't be disappointed though—make parfaits (next page) or fruit whips (page 158) instead; they are excellent desserts for the home freezer. Soften homemade ice-creams in the refrigerator for 30 minutes before serving as they tend to be harder than bought ice-creams. Experiment with the flavoured sugars (page 25) instead of vanilla.

Vanilla Ice-Cream

This is the basic method to follow. Use the same method for the flavoured variations below. As this is a rich custard, you can also make it with all milk or half milk and half powdered milk.

> *1 cup (9 fl oz) milk*
> *1$^1/_2$ cups (13 fl oz) cream*
> *$^1/_2$ vanilla bean*
> *2 egg yolks*
> *$^1/_2$ cup (4 oz) caster sugar*

Put the milk, cream and vanilla into a saucepan and slowly bring to the boil. Remove from the heat, take out the vanilla bean and scrape the powdery centre from it into the milk. Beat the egg yolks and sugar together in a bowl until thick. Blend in some of the hot milk. Put the bowl over a saucepan of boiling water and add the rest of the milk. Stir until the custard is thick.

Remove from the heat and allow to cool. Churn according to the instructions given with your ice-cream maker. Serves 6.

Variations:

Chocolate Ice-Cream

Melt 150 g (5 oz) of dark chocolate in the milk mixture. Try chocolate and hazelnut as well.

Almond Ice-Cream

Put $^1/_2$ cup (2 oz) of ground almonds in with the milk mixture and bring to the boil. Pour through a sieve into a pan and press to extract all the milk. Discard the pulp. Continue recipe.

Raspberry Ice-Cream

Make a quantity of Vanilla Ice-Cream. Blend $1^1/_2$ cups (8 oz) of raspberries to a purée and mix into the ice-cream. Put into a plastic container, cover and store in freezer until half an hour before ready to serve. Other fruits to treat this way are all the berry fruits, strawberries, currants, peaches and apricots.

Parfaits

Parfait is a rich dessert made from egg yolks and thick cream, which is why it doesn't crystallise. That means you can pour it directly into a mould, freeze and forget about it. They can also be poured into individual moulds. Keep well covered with cling film. Follow Strawberry Parfait as the base recipe and try other flavourings as well.

Strawberry Parfait

All the berry fruits taste wonderful singly— or try mixing flavours like strawberry and raspberry, or cherry and strawberry.

$^1/_3$ cup (3 oz) caster sugar
3 tablespoons water
4 egg yolks
$1^1/_4$ cups (5 oz) whipped cream
$^2/_3$ cup (5 fl oz) puréed strawberries

Put the sugar and water in a pan and bring to the boil, stirring until the sugar is dissolved. Boil until the bubbles are a small, even size over the surface and the water is looking white and cloudy. A sugar thermometer should register 110°C (220°F). Remove from heat. Quickly beat the egg yolks and then gradually add the hot sugar syrup, beating all the time. Continue whisking until the mixture is cool and the parfait has nearly doubled in size. Fold in the whipped cream and then the strawberry purée. Pour into a mould. It will take 8 to 10 hours to set. Decorate with fresh fruit when serving or pipe a whirl of cream on top. Serves 6.

Mango Parfait

Add $1^1/_2$ cups (13 fl oz) of mango purée instead of strawberry to the basic recipe.

Apricot Parfait

Use $1^1/_2$ cups (13 fl oz) of dried apricot purée. Try dried peaches and pears as well.

Chocolate Parfait

Add 125 g (4 oz) melted dark chocolate poured in instead of the strawberry purée. Stir in lightly to get a marbled effect if liked.

Pawpaw and Passionfruit Parfait

Add 1 cup (9 fl oz) pawpaw (papaya) purée and $^1/_2$ cup (4 fl oz) of passionfruit.

Bread

Most breads and bread doughs freeze well. It makes more sense to freeze the dough as it takes up less space in the freezer. It is best frozen unrisen. Add 50 per cent more yeast than normal to get the best results. Do not leave in freezer for more than 3 months.

The bread dough for Pizza (page 150) makes a good basic bread which you can change according to taste. Use wholemeal flour instead of plain flour or use a mixture. Add ¹/₂ cup (2 oz) chopped walnuts, hazelnuts or olives or a few tablespoons of fines herbes.

Soda Bread

Traditional country bread made without yeast. If you are new to bread making try this first to gain confidence before trying yeast breads.

> 1¹/₃ cups (8 oz) prunes, pitted and chopped
> 2 cups (8 oz) flour
> 2 cups (8 oz) wholemeal flour
> 2 teaspoons salt
> 1 teaspoon sugar
> 1 teaspoon bicarbonate of soda
> ³/₄ teaspoon baking powder
> 1 tablespoon butter
> ¹/₂ cup finely chopped parsley
> 1¹/₂ cups (13 fl oz) buttermilk

Soak the prunes in warm water for half an hour, drain. Sift the flours, salt, sugar, soda and baking powder into a large bowl. Rub the butter in until the mixture resembles breadcrumbs. Stir in the prunes, parsley and then the buttermilk and mix to a soft dough.

Place on a greased baking tray and, with floured hands, form into a 20 cm (8 in.) round. Use a sharp, floured knife to cut a 12 mm (¹/₂ in.) deep cross in the top of the dough. Bake in the oven

at 190°C (375°F) for 45 minutes or until the loaf sounds hollow when tapped on the bottom.

Yoghurt Soda Bread

> 2 cups (18 fl oz) natural yoghurt
> 2 tablespoons honey
> 4 cups (1 lb) mixed-grain flour
> 2 teaspoons salt
> 1 teaspoon bicarbonate of soda
> ¹/₂ teaspoon baking powder
> 2 tablespoons butter
> 2 tablespoons sunflower seeds

Mix the yoghurt and honey together and let the mixture stand until the honey dissolves into the yoghurt.

Sift the flour, salt, soda and baking powder into a bowl. Rub the butter in until the mixture resembles breadcrumbs. Make a well in the centre and add the yoghurt mixture. Gradually mix the dry ingredients with the yoghurt until you have a ball of dough. Knead for a few moments.

Place the dough in a greased 23 × 10 × 7.5 cm (9 × 4 × 3 in.) loaf pan. Make a lengthwise cut down the centre with a floured knife. Sprinkle the sunflower seeds over the top. Bake in the oven at 190°C (375°F) for an hour or until the bottom feels firm when tapped.

Sun-Dried Tomato Bread

> 4 cups (1 lb) flour
> 14 g (¹/₂ oz) dried yeast, dissolved in a little warm water
> 1 teaspoon sugar
> 1¹/₄ cups (11 fl oz) warm water
> 2 tablespoons chopped Sun-Dried Tomatoes (page 88)
> 1 tablespoon chopped marjoram
> 1 tablespoon olive oil
> 1 tablespoon Maldon salt

*S*ift the flour into a large bowl and make a well in the centre. Stir in the dissolved yeast, then the sugar, followed by the warm water. Blend together until it forms a dough. Put it on a floured board and knead until the dough is light and elastic. While doing this, fold in the tomatoes and marjoram. Brush the dough with oil, put in a bowl, cover with a tea-towel and allow to rise in a warm place. It should double its size in 1 to 1½ hours.

Punch the dough down to dispel any air bubbles, shape into a round and place it on a greased baking tray. Smooth the top. Cut a criss-cross pattern on the top with a floured knife. Sprinkle with Maldon salt. Bake in the oven at 200°C (400°F) for about 30 minutes or until the loaf sounds hollow when tapped.

Focaccia with Grapes and Muscatels

A wonderful bread from Italy. It makes your mouth water just imagining the taste of the warm bread and the sweetness of the grapes and muscatels.

²/₃ cup (6 fl oz) milk
14 g (½ oz) dried yeast
3 cups (12 oz) flour
½ cup (4 oz) sugar
1 teaspoon salt
500 g (1 lb) seedless grapes, destalked
220 g (7 oz) muscatels, soaked in
   brandy
2 teaspoons Maldon salt

*W*arm the milk slightly and dissolve the yeast in it.

Freezer Tip: Breadcrumbs freeze well and will keep for 3 months. It is wise to make a large quantity for use when needed. They remain separate when frozen, so it's easy to take out what you need.

Sift the flour into a large bowl and make a well in the centre. Put the sugar, salt and yeast-milk into the centre. Gradually mix the flour with the wet ingredients until you have a ball of sticky dough. Knead for 5 minutes on a floured board until it is light and elastic. Brush the ball with oil, place in a bowl and cover with a tea-towel. Leave in a warm place to rise to double its size—about 1 to 1½ hours.

Punch down the dough and shape into two 20 cm (8 in.) rounds. Place one on a greased baking tray and cover with half the grapes and muscatels. Put the second round of dough on top and decorate with the rest of the grapes and muscatels. Press the grapes into the dough. Leave, covered, in a warm place to rise again. Sprinkle the top with Maldon salt. Bake in the oven at 180°C (350°F) for about 45 minutes or until the loaf sounds hollow when tapped.

Bread with Olives and Cheese

14 g (½ oz) dried yeast
²/₃ cup (6 fl oz) warm water
3 cups (12 oz) flour
1 teaspoon sugar
1 teaspoon salt
220 g (7 oz) black olives, stoned
   and chopped
220 g (7 oz) gruyère or Cheddar
   cheese, diced
1 tablespoon rosemary leaves

*D*issolve the yeast in the water.

Sift the flour into a large bowl and make a well in the centre. Put the sugar, salt and dissolved yeast into the centre. Gradually mix the flour with the wet ingredients until you have a ball of sticky dough. Knead for 5 minutes on a floured board until it is light and elastic. While you are kneading, incorporate the olives, cheese and rosemary into the dough. Brush the ball with oil, place in a bowl and cover with a tea-towel. Leave in a warm place to rise to double its size—about 1 to $1^1/_2$ hours.

Punch down the dough and shape into 4 rounds about 10 cm (4 in.) across. Allow them to rise again, covered, in a warm place. Bake in the oven at 200°C (400°F) for about 45 minutes or until the loaves sound hollow when tapped.

Pumpkin Scones

Scones are easy to make from the pantry and take no time at all once you have practised a few times. You can cut them into circles or squares or bake as one large scone in a round. What nicer treat on a winter's afternoon chatting with friends around the fire!

> 60 g (2 oz) butter
> $^1/_4$ cup (2 oz) caster sugar
> $^1/_2$ cup cooked, mashed pumpkin
> 1 egg
> $2^1/_2$ cups (10 oz) self-raising flour
> $^1/_2$ teaspoon salt
> $^1/_2$ cup (4 fl oz) buttermilk

Cream the butter and sugar. Add the pumpkin and mix thoroughly. Add the egg, sifted flour and salt. Mix to a soft dough with the buttermilk and turn out onto a floured board. Roll out to a thickness of 2 cm ($^3/_4$ in.). Stamp out with a floured 5 cm (2 in.) cutter, or a glass, flouring the cutter each time you use it.

Place them on a lightly greased baking tray, brush with buttermilk and bake at 220°C (425°F) for 15 minutes or until browned. Makes about 20 scones.

Wholemeal Fruit Scones

Another version of these homely favourites. Serve with butter and homemade fruit jellies.

> 2 cups (8 oz) self-raising wholemeal flour
> 2 teaspoons caster sugar
> $^1/_2$ teaspoon salt
> 60 g (2 oz) butter, softened
> 2 tablespoons sultanas
> 1 cup (9 fl oz) buttermilk

Put the flour, sugar and salt into mixing bowl. Add butter, cut into small pieces, and rub into the flour with your fingertips until the mixture looks like coarse breadcrumbs. Mix in the sultanas. Make a well in the centre of flour, and with a fork mix in the buttermilk to make a soft dough.

Turn the mixture onto a floured board and roll out gently until 2 cm ($^3/_4$ in.) thick. Cut into rounds with a scone cutter or a small glass. Place the scones on a greased baking tray. Brush the scones with a little milk. Bake them in a preheated oven 230°C (450°F) 10 to 12 minutes or until golden brown. Remove scones from the oven and place them on a wire rack, covered with a clean tea-towel, until you are ready to use them. Makes about 15 scones.

Biscuits

Don't bother to freeze biscuits but do think about freezing biscuit dough. Just make sure the mixture has one part fat to four parts of flour. Make the biscuit dough and form it into a long sausage shape. Wrap in aluminium foil and freeze. To bake, put the dough in the refrigerator to soften for 30 to 60 minutes and then slice and bake as usual.

Carrot Biscuits

Children love these attractive biscuits. Store in an airtight tin.

2 cups (8 oz) flour
2 teaspoons baking powder
$^1/_2$ teaspoon salt
250 g (8 oz) butter, softened
$^1/_4$ cup (2 oz) Vanilla Sugar
  (page 4)
1 egg
2 cups grated carrot
$^1/_4$ cup (1 oz) slivered almonds
4 tablespoons bran

Sift the flour with the baking powder and salt. Set aside. With an electric beater, cream the butter in a large bowl until soft, then gradually add the sugar and beat until light and fluffy. Add the egg and mix well. Slowly beat in the flour mixture, then the carrot, almonds and bran, beating just until they are combined.

Drop the dough onto greased baking trays in spoonfuls, 5 cm (2 in.) apart. Bake in the oven at 180°C (350°F) for 20 to 25 minutes. Remove the cooked biscuits to a wire rack. Makes about 30.

Hazelnut Biscuits

These biscuits hardly take a minute to make. It is handy to have the dough in the refrigerator to cut off some slices when you feel like a treat.

6 tablespoons hazelnut oil
125 g (4 oz) butter, softened
$^2/_3$ cup (5 oz) sugar
$^1/_4$ teaspoon salt
2 cups (8 oz) self-raising flour
1 egg
$^3/_4$ cup (3 oz) chopped hazelnuts

Mix together the oil, butter, sugar, salt and flour in a large bowl. Bind with the egg and add the hazelnuts. Form into a roll and chill in the refrigerator for a few hours or days. Slice into thin rounds and bake on a greased baking tray at 190°C (375°F), until they are lightly browned. Cool on a wire rack.

Chocolate and Walnut Biscuits

Use white, light or dark chocolate to coat these biscuits or even a combination. Dribble white chocolate over dark chocolate topping for an extra special occasion. These biscuits will keep several weeks if it is possible to hide them.

2 cups (8 oz) flour
$^1/_2$ teaspoon baking powder
$^1/_2$ cup (4 oz) sugar
125 g (4 oz) butter, softened
1 egg
1 cup (4 oz) walnuts, chopped
90 g (3 oz) chocolate

Sift the flour and baking powder into a large bowl. Mix in the sugar. Put in the butter and mix into the flour with your fingers. When it resembles breadcrumbs, add the egg to bind the dough together. Add the walnuts and mix well. Shape into a log and then cut 10 slices crosswise. Cut the rounds in half. Put them on a greased baking tray and bake in the oven at 160°C (325°F) for about 25 minutes or until crisp and slightly browned. Cool on a wire rack.

Melt the chocolate in a double boiler and brush the top of the biscuits with it. Makes 20.

Oatmeal Triangles

1¹/₄ cup (5 oz) flour
1 teaspoon baking powder
1¹/₂ cups (4 oz) rolled oats
¹/₂ cup (2 oz) wheatgerm
1 cup (9 fl oz) olive oil
¹/₂ cup (6 oz) honey
¹/₂ cup (4 oz) sugar
1 egg
¹/₂ cup (4 fl oz) buttermilk

Put the flour, baking powder, rolled oats and wheatgerm into a large bowl. Mix together well. Heat the oil, honey and sugar together in a pan until they blend with each other. Mix the egg and milk into the bowl with the flour and oats. Then add the honey mixture.

Pour the mixture into a greased 19 × 25 × 2 cm (7¹/₂ × 10 × ³/₄ in.) baking tray. Bake in the oven at 180°C (350°F) for an hour or until crisp on top and firm. Cool on a wire rack. Leave for a day in the refrigerator before cutting into triangles. Cut into squares first, then cut across to form a triangle. Makes about 20.

Cakes

Cake is always handy to have in the pantry for unexpected guests and your hungry family. These dense fruit cakes will actually last for years.

Stained-Glass Cake

Serve this delectable cake in thin slices so that the translucence of the glacé fruits give it the stained glass effect. Store and serve direct from the refrigerator.

1 cup (4 oz) chopped glacé pineapple
1 cup (4 oz) chopped glacé pears
¹/₂ cup (2 oz) glacé cherries, halved
¹/₂ cup (2 oz) chopped glacé apricots
1 cup (5 oz) sultanas
¹/₂ cup (2 oz) walnuts, halved
¹/₂ cup (3 oz) almonds, halved
4 eggs
1 cup (4 oz) flour
¹/₂ cup (4 oz) Vanilla Caster Sugar (page 4)
1 teaspoon allspice
1 teaspoon ground cinnamon
1 teaspoon grated nutmeg
2 tablespoons sherry

Combine all the fruit and nuts in a bowl. Beat the eggs. Add in all the other ingredients, stirring until well mixed. Spoon into a greased and paper-lined cake tin and press down firmly. Bake in a preheated oven at 150°C (300°F) for about 1¹/₂ hours. Test with a skewer—if it comes out clean, the cake is ready. Leave the cake to cool in the tin, turn it out, then wrap it up in aluminium foil and refrigerate for 12 hours. Remove from tin, peel away paper and keep refrigerated.

Stained Glass Cake (this page) is full of glacé fruit and nuts and will last for ages. When assembling the cake, don't forget to keep some whole walnuts and glacé fruits to decorate the top.

167

Christmas Cake

2 cups (10 oz) sultanas
2 cups (10 oz) seedless raisins
1 cup (5 oz) currants
$^1/_2$ cup (3 oz) prunes
$^1/_2$ cup (3 oz) mixed citrus peel
$^1/_2$ cup (3 oz) glacé pineapple
$^1/_4$ cup (2 oz) glacé apricots
$^1/_4$ cup (1 oz) slivered almonds
$^1/_2$ cup (4 fl oz) dark sherry
$^1/_2$ cup (4 fl oz) brandy
1 cup (7 oz) butter
1 cup (7 oz) Vanilla Sugar
  (page 4)
6 eggs
1 tablespoon golden syrup
$2^1/_2$ cups (10 oz) flour, sifted
1 teaspoon cardamom
1 teaspoon ground ginger
1 teaspoon ground cinnamon
1 teaspoon grated nutmeg
$^1/_4$ teaspoon ground cloves
$^1/_2$ teaspoon bicarbonate of soda
$^1/_2$ teaspoon salt
Whole almonds, halved

Chop the fruit and macerate in half the sherry and brandy for 24 hours. Cream the butter and sugar until light and fluffy. Add the eggs, one by one, then add the golden syrup and half the fruit and slivered almonds. Add half the flour and the spices, soda and salt; mix well. Incorporate the rest of the sherry and brandy and the remainder of the flour, fruit and slivered almonds. Butter the cake tin and line it with buttered brown paper. Spoon in the cake mixture. Decorate the top with the halved almonds. Bake in a preheated oven at 180°C (350°F) for $^1/_2$ hour. Turn the oven down to 150°C (300°F), cover the top of the cake with greased brown paper and bake for a further $2^1/_2$ to 3 hours. When the cake is cooked (a toothpick will come out clean), remove it from the tin immediately and wrap aluminium foil around it, then 5 layers of newspaper, so that it cools very slowly. Tie with string and leave in a cool place. After you have first cut it, store in an airtight tin.

Black Treacle Cake

A rich, dark cake that will last for weeks in a cake tin. If you can't get black treacle, use golden syrup instead.

$^2/_3$ cup (5 oz) butter
$^2/_3$ cup (4 oz) dark brown sugar
2 eggs
2 cups (8 oz) flour
1 teaspoon Quatre-Epices (page 43)
1 teaspoon ground ginger
1 teaspoon salt
1 cup (10 oz) black treacle
$^2/_3$ cup (3 oz) hazelnuts, chopped
$^1/_2$ teaspoon bicarbonate of soda
4 tablespoons warm milk

Beat the butter until it is light and fluffy. Add the sugar and beat until it is light. Beat in the eggs, one at a time. Fold in the flour, spices and salt. Then stir in the black treacle and hazelnuts. Add the bicarbonate of soda to the milk and gently stir into the cake mixture. Grease a 20 cm (8 in.) cake tin. Pour the mixture in and place in a preheated oven 180°C (350°F). Bake for $1^1/_2$ hours. If the top is getting too brown, turn the temperature down for the last half hour. Remove from heat. After 10 minutes, turn the cake out onto a rack.

Panforte

A delicious Italian concoction—part cake, part sweetmeat. Whatever it is, it's delicious with bitter coffee or an apéritif.

1¼ cups (14 oz) honey
1¼ cups (9 oz) Vanilla Caster
  Sugar (page 4)
1 cup (5 oz) sultanas
½ cup (3 oz) dried figs
½ cup (3 oz) almonds, skinned
½ cup (3 oz) hazelnuts
½ cup (3 oz) unsalted pistachio
  nuts
2 cups (8 oz) flour
1 tablespoon cocoa
1 tablespoon cinnamon
Icing sugar for dusting

Put the honey and sugar in a pan and stir until sugar is dissolved. Bring to the boil and keep boiling until the mixture begins to darken. Remove from heat. Combine all the other ingredients except the icing sugar in a bowl, pour in the sugar syrup and mix well.

Line a baking tray with baking paper and put the mixture on it. Pat down the mixture until it is evenly 2.5 cm (1 in.) deep and square-shaped. Put into a preheated oven 150°C (300°F) and bake for 45 minutes. Turn out onto a rack. When cool, cut into strips or squares and dust with icing sugar. Store on waxed kitchen paper in an airtight tin. Wrap each piece in cellophane and twist the ends when giving as a gift.

Spice Cake

A beautiful, old-fashioned spice cake to eat for afternoon tea. Sprinkle the top with icing sugar or a mixture of cinnamon and desiccated coconut.

½ cup (2 oz) almonds, chopped
1 cup (4 oz) flour
1 teaspoon baking powder
1 teaspoon ground ginger
1 teaspoon Quatre-Epices (page 43)
½ cup (5 oz) golden syrup
1 egg yolk

Put all the dry ingredients into a bowl and mix well. Heat the golden syrup a little to make it runny. Put a well in the middle of the flour and add the golden syrup and egg. Mix together thoroughly. Spoon the mixture into a greased, small loaf pan. Bake in the oven at 160°C (325°F) for about 45 minutes. Test with a toothpick—if it comes out clean, the cake is ready.

Pound Cake

Made traditionally from one pound each of butter, sugar, eggs and flour. This cake will taste delicious with homemade fruit jams and preserves. You can turn it into a currant cake by adding 3 cups (1 lb) of currants after the flour.

2 cups (1 lb) butter, softened
1 teaspoon salt
2 cups (1 lb) caster (superfine)
  sugar
8 eggs
4 cups (1 lb) flour, sifted

Cream the butter and salt until the butter is very pale. Slowly add the sugar to the butter. Beat in the eggs, one at a time as each is incorporated into mixture. Add the flour a little faster.

Pour the batter into a greased 23 × 20 × 7.5 cm (9 × 8 × 3 in.) cake tin. Bake the cake in the oven at 180°C (350°F) for 45 minutes or until a tooth-pick comes out clean. Let it cool in the pan for 10 minutes then turn it out onto a wire rack.

Chocolate and Almond Cake

This is a very rich cake that will keep well. For a special treat, brush the top with melted chocolate when cool and decorate with halved almonds.

> $^3/_4$ cup (3 oz) flour
> $^3/_4$ cup (3 oz) ground almonds
> 250 g (8 oz) butter
> 7 eggs, separated
> $^3/_4$ cup (8 oz) chocolate powder or cocoa
> $1^1/_4$ cups (8 oz) Vanilla Caster Sugar (page 4)
> $^1/_2$ teaspoon salt

Mix the flour and ground almonds together in a large bowl. Beat the butter until it is a pale yellow, then gradually beat in the egg yolks one at a time. Mix in the chocolate powder, then the sugar and salt. Now add half the flour and almond mixture.

Beat the eggwhites until stiff and fold half gently into the batter. Stir the remaining flour and almond mixture into the batter. Fold in the remaining eggwhites and lightly mix. Pour into a greased 23 cm (9 in.) cake tin, well buttered and lined with greased paper extending 12 mm ($^1/_2$ in.) above the top of the tin. Bake in the oven at 160°C (325°F) for $1^1/_2$ hours. Leave to cool in the turned-off oven. Leave in the tin until it is cold.

Bread Cake

A thrifty but tasty way to use up all the scraps of bread in the pantry and freezer.

> 4 teaspoons butter
> $2^1/_2$ cups (10 oz) fine breadcrumbs
> 8 eggs, separated
> 1 cup (7 oz) caster sugar

> 2 tablespoons sultanas, soaked in brandy
> 4 tablespoons mixed citrus peel
> Grated rind of 1 orange
> $^1/_4$ teaspoon salt
> $^1/_2$ teaspoon lemon juice
> Icing sugar to decorate

Grease a deep cake tin and sprinkle some of the breadcrumbs around the bottom and sides of the tin.

Put the egg yolks and sugar into a large mixing bowl and beat until pale and foamy. Add the rest of the breadcrumbs a little at a time, mixing all the while. Then gently stir in the drained sultanas, citrus peel, orange rind and salt.

Whisk the eggwhites with the lemon juice until they are stiff. Gently fold them into the breadcrumb mixture. When mixed, pour it into the cake tin and bake in the oven at 180°C (350°F) for about 45 minutes. Let it cool a few minutes then turn it out of the tin. Sieve icing sugar over the top.

Sweetmeats

A few homemade sweets that are handy to have in the pantry for children or to serve with coffee. These sweetmeats all last pretty well.

Almond Brittle

An old-fashioned sweetmeat, this almond brittle, or praline, can also be made with walnuts or hazelnuts. To be extra special, you can also pour in 4 tablespoons of kirsch instead of the water. For praline powder, pour the mixture out on a greased baking tray. When it cools and hardens, break it up and reduce it to a powder in the food processor. Store in a screw-top jar.

1 cup (5 oz) unblanched almonds
$^1/_2$ cup (4 oz) sugar
4 tablespoons water or kirsch

Put all the ingredients into a pan over a low heat. Gently stir until the sugar is dissolved. Turn the heat up and boil rapidly until the syrup gradually darkens and the nuts pop. They are ready when they do. Quickly put the pan into an oven tin of iced water to prevent any further cooking. Put spoonfuls at intervals onto greased baking trays. When they are cool, you can lift them up and store on layers of waxed kitchen paper in an airtight tin.

Chocolate Walnut Rocks

75 g ($2^1/_2$ oz) bitter dark chocolate, broken into pieces
6 teaspoons unsalted butter
3 cups (12 oz) walnuts, roughly chopped

Melt the chocolate and butter in a bowl placed in simmering water. Add the walnuts, stir and remove bowl from heat. Keep stirring until the mixture is cool enough to touch and has thickened. Form the mixture into rock-like shapes. Put onto waxed kitchen paper and leave in the refrigerator to set. Store in an airtight tin.

Apricot Jellies

1.5 kg (3 lb) apricots, halved, stoned and chopped
2 tablespoons lemon juice
Caster sugar to measure
Granulated sugar for coating

Put the apricots and lemon into a bowl. Crush the apricots with a potato masher. Leave to macerate for 12 hours. Put the pulp into a pan and bring slowly to the boil. Let it simmer for half an hour or until the fruit is very tender. Purée in a food processor. Measure the purée into a pan and for every 2 cups of purée add one cup of caster sugar. Put the pan on the heat and simmer until the sugar dissolves. Bring the mixture to the boil and boil for about 30 minutes or until the mixture is very thick. Pour the mixture into a greased gratin dish—the mixture should be about 2 cm (1 in.) thick. Let it stand for 12 hours. Cut the paste into bite-size squares and roll in granulated sugar. Let them dry for a few days on a rack in a cool, airy place. Store on waxed kitchen paper in an airtight tin.

Caramelised Hazelnuts

185 g (6 oz) shelled hazelnuts
1 cup (6 oz) icing sugar
$5^1/_2$ tablespoons brandy
$1^1/_2$ tablespoons butter

Put the hazelnuts, sugar and brandy into a pan. Cook over a high heat until the brandy is evaporated. Reduce the heat and simmer until it begins to caramelise. Take off the heat and stir in the butter. Pour onto an oiled baking tray and cool. Break into bite-size pieces and store in an airtight tin on layers of greaseproof paper.

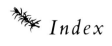

Index

Page numbers in **bold** face indicate illustrations.